FEELING BETTER
CBT WORKBOOK *for teens*

FEELING BETTER
CBT WORKBOOK
for teens

ESSENTIAL SKILLS AND ACTIVITIES TO HELP YOU
MANAGE MOODS, BOOST SELF-ESTEEM,
AND CONQUER ANXIETY

Rachel L. Hutt, PhD

ALTHEA
PRESS

Interior and Cover Designer: Jamison Spittler
Editor: Nana K. Twumasi
Production Editor: Erum Khan

Author photo © Irene Blazquez

ISBN: Print 978-1-64152-332-5 | eBook 978-1-64152-333-2

Printed in Canada

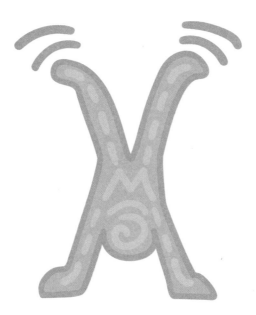

*This workbook is dedicated to
teenagers everywhere.
I know life is hard,
but it will get better.*

CONTENTS

A LETTER TO TEENS

Dear Teens,

I work with many teenagers and know how hard life can be these days. It's incredibly complicated to balance all the demands you have as school gets more challenging, as you want to become more independent from your family, and as friendships become even more difficult to navigate. You don't have to have it all figured out on your own. There are so many others like you who have struggled in life and come out the other side. Sometimes we just need to learn some new ways to live, and get a boost in working hard to achieve the things we want in life. Don't give up and give in to a life that you are not happy with. It is hard to make changes, but I will help you every step of the way. You can do this, just like many teens before you! It takes strength and bravery to recognize when something isn't working and to seek out ways to change it. You've already taken the first step, and this workbook will give you many more steps to take to make the changes you want and need. This book is for you.

Warmly,

Rachel Hutt

A LETTER TO PARENTS

Dear Parents,

As you may remember from your own life, being a teenager is really hard. In fact, being a teen today is even harder than when we were young. Smartphones, social media, and the endless expanses of the Internet have created a new world to grow up in, one that moves at a breakneck speed. It opens up teens to more challenges, stress, demands, and pressures than we had to deal with. It's important to remember that although your teen may be struggling, they are doing the best they can with the tools they have. After giving this book to your teen, perhaps check in with them and see if they are willing to discuss some of the skills they learned—and accept it if they are not. It's hard being the parent of a teen, especially if your teen is struggling. As you support your teen, be sure to get outside support yourself. The skills in this book can be helpful for both you and your teen. Life is not easy these days, but I am presenting you with these tools to help you and your teen survive and thrive.

All the best,

Rachel Hutt

SECTION 1

CBT BASICS

This section discusses the ways Cognitive Behavioral Therapy (CBT) can help you better manage the areas in your life that have been challenging for you, with some exercises along the way. We'll talk about what types of changes you may want to make and identify the values that matter most to you. The section also includes some questions to help you understand how you are doing right now and figure out where you might want to focus your work.

WHAT DO YOU WANT TO CHANGE?

Congratulations on taking a big step toward making changes just by opening this book!

Life as a teen can be hard and stressful, and you might not know how to make it better. You may have challenges in school, with friends, in romantic relationships, and with your family. You might be putting in a lot of effort to make things better, but some parts of life still aren't quite the way you want them to be.

The hard truth is that many of the skills you need to make the most out of your life are not taught in school. Often it may seem like life is a series of expectations: to know how to be happier, get along with others, bring up your grades, manage daily stress, be nice to your family, or simply let go of the things that upset you. But none of these are easy! It takes skills and practice to successfully work through these types of situations, at all ages. The good news is that you can learn these skills, starting now.

Cognitive Behavioral Therapy (CBT) provides skills and tools to help you in all parts of your life, regardless of your unique circumstances. CBT will help you manage your emotions, thoughts, and behaviors so you can feel, think, and act more like the person you want to be. You may know what it feels like to be hijacked by intense emotions, worries, or urges—in this workbook you'll learn how you can overcome those experiences. You'll discover how you can make the changes you've always wanted to make and how to get out of the loops that have been keeping you stuck. Learning these skills will help you avoid situations you don't want, such as conflicts with friends, problems in relationships, mood swings, intense negative emotions, obsessive worries, low self-esteem, or impulsive behaviors that get you into trouble. Instead, you will be able to put yourself in situations you do want that make your life better.

Whether a parent, teacher, counselor, or therapist gave you this book, or you happened to find it yourself, remember that this book is *yours* and this program is for *you*—no one else. You get to choose how you use this book, what you want to change, and how you want to live your life. Your parents, friends, and teachers may want certain things for you, but you are the one who ultimately gets to decide.

The first step in figuring out how to live the life you want is to determine your values. **Values** are the principles that guide you and help you become the person you want to be. One example of a value is being a good friend. **Goals** are the concrete steps you take to express your values. So if your value is being a good friend, one goal you could set might be to make time to hang out with a friend who's having a hard time. It's important to identify your values and then regularly set goals in line with those values.

Here are some exercises to start the process. Remember that it is your job to figure out what *your* values are, not what your parents or teachers tell you your values *should be*. Think about what you believe is important. It may be something your parents taught you or it might be totally different from their values. What's important is that these values are consistent with who *you* are and who *you* want to be.

EXERCISE: IDENTIFYING VALUES

Here are some values that may be important for you. Consider each one, and then write in your own ideas on the blank lines at the end of the list:

- Be a good friend
- Put family first
- Volunteer and help others
- Be independent
- Enjoy life
- Always try to learn and grow
- Lead others
- Live a healthy lifestyle
- Have integrity
- Have honest and trusting relationships
- Be fair and treat people equally
- Act responsibly and reliably
- Be adventurous and try new things
- Be curious and nonjudgmental
- Accomplish goals

- _____

- _____

- _____

- _____

Of the preceding values, pick three to five values that are the most important to you. Then rank them based on your current priorities. They can all be important, but consider the values you're most interested in working toward *right now*.

As you go through the workbook, keep these top values in mind. They will act as your guide for using certain skills for your needs, and for choosing behaviors to work on in the behavior section.

1. _____

__ _____

__ _____

__ _____

__ _____

Both exercises adapted from Rathus, Jill H., and Alec L. Miller. *DBT Skills Manual for Adolescents*. New York: The Guilford Press, 2015.

CBT is a type of therapy that includes many ideas, tools, and principles that teach you how to face all kinds of challenges. CBT is unique in that it reflects what is happening in the present moment and looks at the connection between your thoughts, emotions, and behaviors.

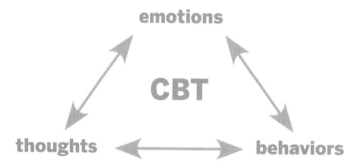

You can think about CBT like a triangle, where each point has a focus. One point is emotions, one point is thoughts, and one point is behaviors. Let's say you have to give a presentation in a class. The emotion you experience could be fear or anxiety about standing up in front of your class. You may have thoughts such as "I will sound so ignorant," "I won't know what I am talking about," or "Everyone will be watching and judging me." To avoid this, you might pretend to be sick in the morning, you might freeze before or during the presentation, talk really quickly or quietly just to get it over with, or run and hide in the bathroom during the class—these are behaviors. You may have these experiences in a different order—you may feel fear, have the thoughts, and engage in the behavior, or you might stumble over your words (another behavior) and then experience the negative thoughts and experience fear. The point is that they are all interconnected.

Although these three points on the triangle feed off of each other, we can also use this interconnectedness to learn how to better manage our challenges. This is the core of what CBT does. By knowing how to improve each one of these areas, you can improve the other ones. You can learn to lower the emotional intensity before negative thoughts pop up. You can learn to let thoughts go or evaluate them without automatically believing them and acting on them. And you can practice ways to change troubling behaviors so you don't have unwanted thoughts and emotions.

This workbook has a section dedicated to each of these important aspects of CBT—thoughts, behaviors, and emotions. One by one, we will focus on specific strategies to target each area, and learn how they work together. From there, you'll learn how to pick tools and strategies to better handle different situations at school, at home, and with your peers.

WHAT IS CBT GOOD FOR?

CBT has been scientifically proven to effectively treat many different types of common problems that people have. Take a look at this list and see if you can relate to any of these.

For people with anxiety, CBT can help them:

- Experience less worry
- Be less bothered by worries when they naturally arise
- Face difficult situations
- Face social situations with less fear

For people with depression, CBT can help them:

- Get unstuck from the past
- Engage with life and socialize more often
- Get a wider perspective on life, instead of assuming everything that happens will always be negative

For people with unhealthy eating behaviors, CBT can help them:

- Change the way they relate to food and change their eating behaviors
- Change troublesome thoughts related to foods and body shape
- Improve their body image

For people with obsessive thoughts and compulsive behaviors, CBT can help them:

- Put a stop to acting on those compulsive behaviors
- Break free of obsessive thought loops

CBT has also been shown to help other types of challenges, such as problems with attention, focus, and organization; chronic physical pain or headaches; trauma or traumatic experiences; seeing or hearing things that might not be there; and sleep problems. Though you will be able to use some of the content in this workbook to address aspects of some of those problems, this workbook may not be sufficient to completely treat those problems. You may want to seek the help of a psychologist or counselor who specializes in working with people with these problems (see more resources at the end of this section).

In general, CBT has been shown to help with difficulty managing emotions, thoughts, and behaviors that sometimes lead to bigger, unwanted problems, such as constant worrying or rumination, avoidance, problems in relationships, withdrawal from friends and family, problematic eating behaviors, dependence on drugs or alcohol, sleep problems, or trouble in school.

I've seen firsthand how helpful CBT can be for teens. I have worked with teens who were initially anxious about taking tests, talking in class, and handing in assignments, but with CBT they became much more comfortable and able to face these situations with confidence. I have worked with teens who came in depressed and stuck on thoughts and beliefs that were getting in their way, and I have watched them become happier, build a life that they enjoy, and become disentangled from the thoughts that bogged them down. I have seen teens build stable and satisfying friendships, and try dating in a way that feels safe and exciting for them. I have worked with teens who went from feeling uncomfortable in social situations to enjoying going to parties, dances, and being in large groups. I have also watched teens change the way they speak to others, change the way they treat themselves, and change their behavior for the better in school and at home.

HOW CAN CBT HELP YOU?

There is no one way CBT works—the key is figuring out what you would like to take from it. As such, this workbook will only be as helpful as you make it. The best way to make it useful is to understand the areas in life where you're in need of some help.

For instance, reflect on your emotions. Are you someone who reacts more quickly or more frequently to emotional situations than other people? Do you think you feel emotions more intensely than other people? Does it take you longer to calm down when you get upset than other people? If you have these types of emotional tendencies, it can be difficult to know how to deal with all of the emotional reactions you experience. People may tell you to get over your emotions, just deal with the situation, not overreact, or let it go. This can feel confusing or isolating. It may be because other people don't understand the way your emotions work. In section 4, we'll examine different ways to manage the emotional reactions you have and how to prevent these emotional reactions from interfering with your life and relationships.

Do you have some challenges with self-esteem and self-image? Sometimes this can lead to problems with expressing yourself to others or having satisfying relationships. It's hard to feel good with other people when you are uncomfortable with yourself. Low self-esteem is often related to our thoughts and behaviors. When we think negatively about ourselves, it affects our emotions and also results in behaviors in line with those beliefs. For instance, if you believe that you are not as smart as your friends, you might feel sad and then not study for a test. Then, if you bomb the test, you may keep believing you are not as smart. However, if you had thought about yourself differently, you may have felt more confident, put in the effort to study, and done well on the test. In other words: When we learn to catch the problematic or troublesome thoughts, we gain the opportunity to change our behavior, become more assertive with others, and improve our overall self-esteem.

To get the most out of this workbook, it's important for you to figure out and prioritize the behaviors and thought patterns you would like to change. CBT can help you get more organized in these ideas and start to break down steps and goals that may at first seem overwhelming or unattainable.

This workbook will help you assess where you currently are, take you through the different areas of CBT, and teach you the skills you need to improve in your own life circumstances. Knowing yourself—and your strengths and challenges—is the first step.

SO, HOW ARE YOU DOING?

You may be very aware of some of the problems you are facing and what you would like to change. Or you may just be unhappy and unsure of what is going on or why. This section will help you assess where you are right now. We will examine three areas: self-esteem, worry and anxiety, and sadness and depression. Remember that this is just a starting point. By assessing where you are now, you can then help yourself get to the place you want to be.

Self-Esteem

Self-esteem has to do with how you feel about yourself. It concerns your self-worth, your competency, and your unique traits. People with low self-esteem tend to see all their flaws and ignore their strengths, and believe that they are not worthy of love, attention, compliments, or anything positive from others. Often people with low self-esteem avoid the spotlight, tend to feel down or lonely, or may be irritable and aggressive. If you have low self-esteem, you may believe that people can see through you as an imposter or a phony. Low self-esteem can interfere with the kind of relationships you want, and prevent you from taking risks, trying new things, speaking up about something, or taking on a leadership role.

EXERCISE: SELF-ESTEEM ASSESSMENT

Here is an assessment of your self-esteem. Check whether each statement is never true, sometimes true, or often true.

	NEVER	SOMETIMES	OFTEN
1. I respect myself.	☐	☐	☐
2. I feel confident.	☐	☐	☐
3. I feel satisfied with myself.	☐	☐	☐
4. I believe I am good enough.	☐	☐	☐
5. I feel proud of myself.	☐	☐	☐
6. I believe I am just as worthy as other people.	☐	☐	☐
7. I feel comfortable in different settings.	☐	☐	☐
8. I feel useful.	☐	☐	☐
9. I meet my goals.	☐	☐	☐
10. I think positively about myself.	☐	☐	☐
11. I believe I am just as good as my friends.	☐	☐	☐
12. I can think of my good qualities.	☐	☐	☐

Adapted from Rosenberg, Morris. *Society and the Adolescent Self-Image*. Princeton, NJ: Princeton University Press, 1965.

If you placed the most checks in the "never" column, you may have notable challenges with self-esteem. And if you checked "never" a few times, or "sometimes" several times, you likely experience some problems with your self-esteem. Keep this in mind as you go through the workbook, as it includes several exercises that specifically address self-esteem challenges.

Worry and Anxiety

While worrying is part of having anxiety, it's important to understand the difference between worry and anxiety. Worry is a type of thinking that has to do with consistently anticipating the future in a negative way and not being able to focus on and live in the present moment. It can result in difficulty concentrating, irritability, restlessness, and feeling on edge. You might be a worrier if you are always thinking "what if," if you always consider the worst-case scenario, and if things always seem like they will be worse than they actually are. Some worrying is normal and we all do it, but spending a large part of the day and night worrying can cause problems. CBT can help you better respond to these thoughts and worry less as a result.

Worry is one part of anxiety, but in addition to worry, anxiety includes physical symptoms such as panic, muscle tension, trouble breathing, aches and pains, teeth grinding, and stomach problems. It might also include behaviors related to avoidance or spending way too much time on something. Although just having a lot of worry can take a toll on your happiness and result in problems, the added stress of anxiety can interfere with your life and lead to more serious physical problems, as well as behavioral problems such as missing school or not doing homework, not socializing, and not doing certain activities you enjoy.

EXERCISE: ANXIETY ASSESSMENT

Here is an assessment of your current anxiety level. Check whether each statement is never true, sometimes true, or often true.

	NEVER	SOMETIMES	OFTEN
1. I spend a lot of the day worrying.	☐	☐	☐
2. I have a hard time controlling my worry.	☐	☐	☐
3. I have a hard time calming down.	☐	☐	☐
4. I have trouble concentrating.	☐	☐	☐
5. I feel irritable.	☐	☐	☐
6. I have trouble falling or staying asleep at night.	☐	☐	☐
7. I avoid situations when I am anxious or worried.	☐	☐	☐
8. I worry about how others will view me.	☐	☐	☐
9. I try to do things perfectly.	☐	☐	☐
10. There are specific situations I avoid or experience a lot of fear in.	☐	☐	☐

Adapted from Spielberger, Charles D., C. D. Edwards, J. Montouri, and R. Lushene. "State-Trait Anxiety Inventory for Children." *PsycTESTS Dataset*, 1973. doi:10.1037/t06497-000.

If you placed the most checks in the "often" column, you may have notable challenges with anxiety. And if you checked "often" a few times, or "sometimes" several times, you likely experience worry or some aspects of anxiety. At any level, CBT can help you reduce worry and anxiety. If you checked "often" on most of the questions, you may want to consider asking for professional help in navigating your anxiety, especially if you don't notice a lot of changes after trying to use the workbook.

Sadness and Depression

Feeling sad, down, or blue once in a while is completely normal, especially during your teenage years. But some people feel sad more often than not. They find that they are not enjoying things they used to or start withdrawing from family and friends. These might be signs of depression. Other signs include sleep problems, changes in appetite, difficulty concentrating, low energy or fatigue, and having a lot of negative thoughts about yourself, the world, and your future. Some people with depression can feel more irritable than sad but can still be depressed. Depression may start out at a low level, but before you know it, it's hard to wake up in the morning, hard to get to school, hard to do homework, hard to talk to others, and hard to even take a shower.

EXERCISE: DEPRESSION ASSESSMENT

Here is an assessment to get a better sense of your level of depression. Choose whether each statement was never true, sometimes true, or often true **during the past week.**

DURING THE PAST WEEK	NEVER	SOMETIMES	OFTEN
1. I felt sad for most of the day.	☐	☐	☐
2. I felt irritable for most of the day.	☐	☐	☐
3. I couldn't enjoy things I usually enjoy.	☐	☐	☐
4. I had trouble concentrating.	☐	☐	☐
5. I wasn't very hungry.	☐	☐	☐
6. I slept more than usual.	☐	☐	☐
7. I felt like crying.	☐	☐	☐
8. I felt hopeless.	☐	☐	☐
9. I had trouble sleeping.	☐	☐	☐
10. I believed bad things were going to happen.	☐	☐	☐
11. I felt alone or lonely.	☐	☐	☐
12. I withdrew from friends or family.	☐	☐	☐
13. I had less energy than usual.	☐	☐	☐
14. I had less motivation than usual.	☐	☐	☐
15. I felt like nothing worked out the way I wanted.	☐	☐	☐

Adapted from Shahid, Azmeh, Kate Wilkinson, Shai Marcu, and Colin M. Shapiro, eds. "Center for Epidemiological Studies Depression Scale for Children (CES-DC)." In *STOP, THAT and One Hundred Other Sleep Scales*, 93–96. New York: Springer, 2011. doi:10.1007/978-1-4419-9893-4_16.

If you checked "often" the most, you may have notable challenges with depression. And if you checked "often" a few times, or "sometimes" several times, you may be experiencing bouts of sadness or aspects of depression. CBT can help you reduce sadness and depression. If you checked "often" on most of the questions, you may want to consider asking for professional help in navigating some signs of depression, especially if you don't notice a lot of changes after trying the exercises and practices in the workbook.

DO YOU NEED MORE HELP?

Remember that this workbook alone may not be enough to give you the help you need. If you are struggling with suicidal thoughts or urges, self-harm, alcohol dependence, drugs, or other impulsive or destructive behaviors, it's important to get professional help. Or, if you try this workbook and it doesn't give you the changes you're looking for, you may also want outside support. Start by talking to an adult you trust: a parent, teacher, school counselor, coach, or a friend's parent. Let them know what is going on (share as much as you're comfortable with) and ask if they can help you find a mental health professional.

If you want to start looking for a professional on your own, or need someone right now, here are some resources:

The National Suicide Prevention Lifeline is available 24 hours every day by phone at 1-800-273-8255 or by using an online chat.

The Trevor Project also offers a hotline, chat, text support, and other online resources, geared directly to teens within the LGBTQ spectrum. They are available at 1-866-488-7386.

If it is an emergency for your safety, call 911 or walk into the nearest hospital emergency room.

If you are looking for a psychologist or counselor who uses the same approach as this workbook, you or your parents can look up therapists in your area through the Association for Behavioral and Cognitive Therapies' therapist directory: http://www.findcbt.org/xFAT.

WRAP UP

In this section, you learned about CBT and the ways it can help you become the person you want to be, as well as what you can expect to get out of this workbook. Here are the main takeaways:

- This workbook will help you with what you want to change in your life, not just what others tell you to change.

- You've identified your values, and these values will help guide you as you progress through the workbook.

- CBT looks at the relationship between your emotions, thoughts, and behaviors, and teaches you skills to improve each area.

- Working on each area will help you improve the other areas as well.

- This workbook will be as helpful as you make it.

- You now have a baseline understanding of how you are doing and perhaps an idea of where you want to focus your efforts. Now we can work on learning the skills to build the life you want!

SECTION 2
YOUR THOUGHTS

In this section, you will learn strategies to allow your thoughts to come and go without getting stuck on them. You will learn about common thought patterns that can lead people to get in trouble or create unwanted consequences. You will learn how to evaluate your thoughts and determine whether they are actually based on facts. You will also learn how to reframe thoughts to help you see things in a different light. And you will have an opportunity to question some beliefs that you have held about yourself that may not be true or helpful.

STICKY THOUGHTS

In the last section, we learned that one of the points on the CBT triangle is *thoughts*. Thoughts are tricky because we have them all day, every day. Our thoughts are always running and can influence us in ways we like and ways we don't. Thoughts are useful when we're working through a problem or trying to make a decision. You may love daydreaming or fantasizing, and you need your thoughts for that. However, thoughts can also be unhelpful—even harmful. They can run in loops, they can be overly negative, they can hurt our self-esteem, and they can distract us from what's happening in the present moment.

Thoughts make up the ongoing conversation we have with ourselves. Some thoughts pop up quickly and are just a few words, phrases, or images. Others can be *really* sticky and difficult to remove, like super glue. When we get stuck on a thought, it can lead to ruminating about the past or worrying about the future. It can be really hard to get unstuck from certain thoughts and focus on the moment. These thoughts are probably not helping us and can actually make us feel worse. Remember, the internal chatter in your mind is not automatically meaningful. You can try to view your thoughts simply as mental events that just happen. It may not feel like it, but you can actually learn to choose whether you stick to your thoughts . . . or just let them come and go.

Think about standing on a busy street waiting for a taxi, rideshare, bus, or parent to pick you up. You watch dozens of cars fly by, but you don't automatically get in the first car you see. You choose your ride carefully, wait for the right car and driver, and then get in the car and go for the ride. We can learn to simply watch our thoughts go by like cars on a street and choose which thoughts we want to ride. This takes a lot of practice, but over time you'll be able to sort out unhelpful thoughts from the helpful ones and take your rides accordingly.

One way to stop sticking to thoughts is by catching the common tricks our minds play on us, which can lead us to take some thoughts at face value when we shouldn't. When this happens, we are actually making a thinking mistake, or "thinking error." These mistakes lead us to make incorrect assumptions about ourselves, our future, and other people. These assumptions can get us in trouble, cause us to hurt others, make us feel bad about ourselves, prevent us from doing things in life we want to do, or create problems at school, with friends, or with family.

Before we look at the common types of thinking errors, let's practice simply allowing thoughts to go by like cars on the road without jumping on them or holding on.

EXERCISE: WATCHING YOUR THOUGHTS GO BY

There are a lot of different ways to practice watching your thoughts go by. Here are a few visualizations to help you allow your thoughts to pass without sticking to them. Practice each one for a minute and find the ones that work best for you:

- Imagine your thoughts as clouds in the sky. You are lying in the grass and your focus is on the blue sky. You don't move with the clouds, you just watch your thoughts on clouds moving across the sky.

- Visualize your thoughts as leaves moving down a stream. You don't run to follow the leaves. You just watch the water and see your thoughts float by.

- Imagine your thoughts as objects on a conveyor belt moving down the line. You don't stop the thoughts from moving or take anything off the belt. They just pass by.

- See your thoughts as captions on a movie screen. You see them coming and going across the screen without pausing the movie.

- Or, if you like the image of cars on the street, you can imagine putting your thoughts on different cars going by while you stand still at the side of the road.

COMMON THINKING ERRORS

Our thoughts can really fool us into assuming that something is true and lead us to make incorrect conclusions. This happens when we exaggerate the threat of a situation, assume that things will always be a certain way, think we are responsible for something even when it has nothing to do with us, see only the negatives in things, or make assumptions about what others are thinking. If we don't notice these thinking mistakes, we can end up with more problems and a lot of unnecessary distress. The best way to avoid this trap is to begin to label some of your thoughts with these types of thinking errors.

On the following pages, you'll find several types of common thinking errors we all make. Your job will be to first identify examples of each type of mind trick that you experience in your own life. The second step is to create an alternate thought that is based on current facts, after recognizing that your mind played a trick on you. For example, if while studying for a test you have thoughts like, "I will fail this test, I will fail the class, and I won't get into college," you would recognize the thinking error, and then create an alternate thought based on what you do know. It could be "I am really worried about this test," "This test only counts for 10 percent of my final grade," or "Other times when I have been worried about tests I have done okay." The important part is to make an alternate thought that is based on facts rather than mind tricks.

All or Nothing

All-or-nothing thinking (sometimes referred to as black-or-white thinking) is when you think that things are either one side of the extreme or the other, with no gray area or middle ground. For example, either someone is your best friend or your worst enemy. If you don't get 100 percent on a test, you basically failed. If one bad thing happens, it means nothing good is happening. To make an alternate thought, find a middle path of the two extremes.

List three examples of all-or-nothing thinking from your life and three alternate thoughts to combat these examples.

1. _____

_____

2. _____

_____

3. _____

_____

1. _____

_____

2. _____

_____

3. _____

_____

Catastrophizing

Catastrophizing is when you believe there will be a catastrophe based on something that happened, and you keep projecting out from that event. For example, if you get a bad grade on a test and catastrophize the situation, you will likely believe a series of false assumptions that can spiral—for example, you will fail that class, which means you won't graduate, you won't get into college, and you will end up living on the streets. Or, if your parents don't let you go to the party, you will miss all the important things; everyone will make new friends and not want to be friends with you; and you will be alone forever. In other words, it's taking one thing and making a whole movie out of it—even though none of the other steps have happened. To create an alternate thought instead, rein in your thinking to focus on what is actually happening—the actual facts.

List three examples of catastrophizing from your life and three alternate thoughts to combat these examples.

1. _____

_____

2. _____

_____

3. _____

_____

1. _____

_____

2. _____

_____

3. _____

_____

Personalization

Personalization is when you believe you are responsible for causing a problem that you had nothing to do with, or that someone said or did something to target you when that may not actually be the case. For example, let's say you believe your friends are not talking to each other because of something you said, you believe your parents are fighting because of you, you believe that the teacher was talking about you directly when they said the class is not doing well, or you think that you did something wrong when your friend told you she can't hang out because her parents won't let her go out. To make an alternate thought, consider any facts (or lack of facts) related to your role in the situation.

List three examples of personalization from your life and three alternate thoughts to combat these examples.

1. _____

_____

2. _____

_____

3. _____

_____

1. _____

_____

2. _____

_____

3. _____

_____

Negative Filtering

Negative filtering is the opposite of rose-colored glasses. You can only see the negatives in situations instead of seeing both the positives and negatives. You ignore information that is not in line with the negative view you have. For example, if you get a 99 percent on a test, you focus instead on the one point you missed instead of the fact that you did very well and got an A. Or if someone gives you a lot of compliments and mentions one thing you could improve on, you only focus on the suggestion to improve and ignore the compliments. Or perhaps one friend does not want to hang out and you forget about the other friends who said they would come to hang out. To make an alternate thought, look again at any information opposite of your view; focus on the positive aspects you know to be true to help balance your outlook.

List three examples of negative filtering from your life and three alternate thoughts to combat these examples.

1. _____

_____

2. _____

_____

3. _____

_____

1. _____

_____

2. _____

_____

3. _____

_____

Overgeneralization

Overgeneralization is when you make a very broad conclusion based on one situation and apply it to many different situations. If something happens once, you believe that it will always happen that way. For example, you had a bad day at school; therefore school is horrible and will *always* be that way. Or, no one asked you to the dance, so that must mean you will *never* have a date or be in a relationship. The trick to catching these is looking for broad generalizing words like *always* or *never*. To make an alternate thought, focus on the details of the present situation and see it for what it is.

List three examples of overgeneralization from your life and three alternate thoughts to combat these examples.

1. _____

_____

2. _____

_____

3. _____

_____

1. _____

_____

2. _____

_____

3. _____

_____

Mind Reading

Mind reading is exactly what it sounds like: You believe you can read minds. You are 100 percent certain that others are thinking something, but you have no facts, or very few facts, to support this. For example, when your friend takes a day to respond to a text message, you assume he is mad at you. When the teacher doesn't say good morning after passing you in the hall, you assume she doesn't like you. When your sibling doesn't ask you before borrowing your laptop, you think they are trying to get back at you for something. To make an alternate thought, check the facts that are observable to others, not just you. Filter out any assumptions. Remind yourself that you have no idea what someone is thinking (unless they tell you).

List three examples of mind reading from your life and three alternate thoughts to combat these examples.

1. _____

_____

2. _____

_____

3. _____

_____

1. _____

_____

2. _____

_____

3. _____

_____

Emotional Reasoning

Emotional reasoning happens when you have strong emotions that can make you believe that your thought is true even when you don't have any evidence—or even have evidence against it. If you feel sad because you were lonely this weekend with nothing to do, your friends must not like you. If you are mad about having too much homework, you must have bad teachers. If you are anxious about going to a party, then something bad will happen and you should stay home. If you are worried about your friend, you must have done something wrong. To make an alternate thought, think about the facts without the emotion—the way a friend would if you talked to them about your thoughts. For example, if you believed something bad would happen at a party because you felt anxious with no other evidence, what would a friend tell you?

List three examples of emotional reasoning from your life and three alternate thoughts to combat these examples.

1. _____

_____

2. _____

_____

3. _____

_____

1. _____

_____

2. _____

_____

3. _____

_____

TESTING YOUR THEORIES

Once you have caught some of these common thinking errors and created alternative thoughts, you may no longer believe in your problematic thoughts. But you might still need to do additional work to get yourself unstuck. Perhaps you changed the thought, and although it makes sense, you still feel like the original thought is true. Or perhaps the original thought seems like it is based on fact so it is hard to even think of another thought. Maybe you did it, felt better, and then a minute later the original thought popped back in again and you have to keep reminding yourself you changed it. In any of these cases, or if doing the previous exercise didn't help, you can use another technique, which I'll talk about here.

Imagine you are a scientist and you have to run an experiment. To do this, you would create a hypothesis for your experiment—but you couldn't assume it was true until you did it. For example, when I was in college I tested whether people walked down a hill faster when they listened to a fast song compared to a slow song. My hypothesis was that people would walk faster with the fast song. What I actually found when I ran the experiment was that girls walked faster to the fast song as I expected, but boys had no difference in their pace. The findings surprised me and showed me that my original assumption wasn't entirely based on facts.

We want to approach thoughts the same way: They are just hypotheses! They are not scientifically proven facts. You need to investigate them before believing them. The first way to do this is to think about what evidence you have. Imagine you are collecting all the facts that you have so far, by looking at evidence in support of your thought as well as evidence against it. Think about this practice as putting your thought on trial and only being able to present observable facts to the jury.

Here's a real-life example to help. One boy I worked with was worried that he would fail a math test, and therefore fail his math class. We created this chart together using evidence *for* his thought and evidence *against*:

I will fail my math test and fail math class.

Evidence For	Evidence Against
▪ Math is my worst subject.	▪ I have a math tutor who has helped me.
▪ I have done poorly on math tests in the past.	▪ I have not failed math class before.
▪ I don't understand the material for the test.	▪ The test is only one grade that goes into my final grade.
▪ My math grade is currently a 77 going into this test.	▪ I did all my assignments that go into my final grade.

From this exercise, we can then rethink the hypothesis that he had going into his math test. We want to take all the evidence for and against to come up with the best hypothesis we have. His new hypothesis was: "Math is really hard for me, I am studying hard with my tutor, and this test won't solely determine my final grade." He felt a lot better going into his math test with this new hypothesis than the previous one.

Now it's your turn. Pick a thought that has given you some trouble and let's see if you can make a new hypothesis for it.

EXERCISE: BEING A SCIENTIST

Thought: _____

_____

Evidence For	Evidence Against
_____	_____
_____	_____
_____	_____
_____	_____

New hypothesis: _____

_____

If it is difficult to come up with any evidence against your thought, you might need some prompting. The following is a list of questions you can ask yourself to help make the most accurate hypothesis about your thought. Using the example of the boy who was worried he would fail his math test and class, look at the questions and his answers that follow in italics. Then for each question, add your own answer about your own thought to the line underneath.

Is there a possible different outcome than the one you are worried about? *Yes, I could pass the test and pass the class, or even not do well on the test and pass the class.*

_____

_____

Am I making assumptions based on my emotions or confusing a feeling with a fact? (In other words, since my emotions are so strong, the thought must be true.) *Maybe.*

_____

What's the likely outcome based on what I already know has happened in past similar situations? *I won't fail but might get a C on the test.*

_____

_____

What is the percentage chance or the odds that my thought is true? 100 percent, 50 percent, 5 percent? *The chances of me actually failing are probably more like 30 percent.*

_____

Has there been a situation in the past similar to this that I got through? How did it turn out? *Yes, I have almost failed math tests before, but I have passed my math classes.*

_____

_____

What's the worst thing that could happen? *I could fail my math class.*

_____

_____

How would I cope with this worst thing happening? *I could go to summer school and make it up.*

_____

_____

Is there another point of view or perspective on this? *I have worked with my tutor and am getting better at math, and might not fail the test or the class.*

_____

_____

Can I see the future? *No.*

_____

What information might I be missing or forgetting about? *I can do extra credit to bring my grade up, and I got a B on the last test.*

_____

_____

HEALTHY BODY, HEALTHY MIND: NUTRITION

Being careful and mindful about what you eat can actually help balance emotions, mood, and behaviors. For instance, if you are hungry, you can become more irritable, experience more negative emotions, become more fatigued, have trouble concentrating and focusing, be less productive, or act more impulsively. This might happen if you are dieting or trying to lose weight in a way that is unhealthy, including restricting what or when you eat, throwing up after eating, following a fad diet that your doctor didn't tell you about, or doing a cleanse. These types of eating behaviors are not healthy or balanced.

Or, you may be someone who eats carelessly, eats too much, or doesn't eat during the day and has a large dinner or a lot of snacks at night. You might sometimes binge on snacks as a result of negative emotions or hunger that you haven't been managing. Eating too much at any given time is also a problem and can result in guilt or shame, physical discomfort, or other impulsive behaviors.

Here are some tips for building better eating habits:

- Have three meals a day and two snacks no more than three or four hours apart for proper digestion, appetite, and energy. Grab a yogurt or granola bar on your way to school. Make sure you can have a snack before dinner. Plan ahead so you aren't stuck with nothing, or with something that isn't good for you.

- Each person's relationship to food is different, so it is important to determine which foods energize you and make you feel good, and which foods make you feel sluggish, tired, and negative. For example, caffeine and sugar affect everyone differently.

- Eat mindfully. This means when you are eating, just eat. Eating mindfully means focusing on your eating and noticing the small details of the taste and texture of each bite. Notice how the food breaks down, the experience of chewing, and the experience of swallowing. This can be a very pleasant activity—especially for your favorite foods—and help slow down your eating so you can more easily stop when you're full.

LEARNING TO REFRAME

Another way to get unstuck from a thought is to see it in a different light or get another perspective on the thought. We call this reframing the thought. Reframing is important because it decreases the emotional intensity the thought may have originally caused, helps you change unwanted behaviors that may have been related to the thought, and can free you from spending so much time focusing on one topic or situation. Let's look at some ways to reframe thoughts with some examples from other teens.

One way to reframe a thought is to consider the advantages and disadvantages of having the thought. Let's look at the example of Liza, who was invited to a party and had this thought: "No one will want to talk to me at the party."

No one will want to talk to me at the party.

Advantages of Having This Thought	Disadvantages of Having This Thought
■ I won't be disappointed.	■ I will go into the party feeling sad.
■ I don't have to make any effort.	■ I may look like I don't want to talk to anyone.
■ I can prepare myself.	■ I may end up missing a party I might have enjoyed.
■ It's okay if I avoid the party.	■ I might miss an opportunity to make new friends.

After doing this exercise, Liza realized that although there were some reasons the thought was helpful, having it went against her goals of facing her anxiety in social situations, trying to enter new situations with an open mind, and making new friends. She realized she also might miss opportunities to have a positive experience. By reframing the thought this way, she was able to see things differently and went to the party feeling more optimistic.

Another tool to examine the different likelihoods of a situation is a pie chart. Let's take Janet. Because her friend Leigh had not responded to Janet's text for several hours, Janet had this thought: "My friend Leigh doesn't like me anymore." First, we brainstormed all the different possible reasons why Leigh had not yet responded to her text. They included: Leigh was mad at Janet; Leigh no longer liked Janet; Leigh was busy doing homework; Leigh was out with her family; Leigh's phone battery had died; Leigh had been grounded and her parents took her phone; Leigh was sick and sleeping much of the day. Then, out of 100 percent, we tried to figure out the probability of each one being true. You can see in the following pie chart how we broke down the different options.

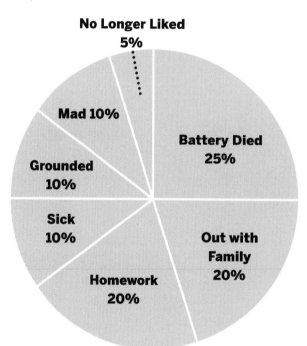

Once Janet saw the pie chart, she realized that it was very unlikely that Leigh no longer liked her anymore. Leigh's phone battery often died by the afternoon, so there was a good chance that was true. Leigh also had a lot of homework she had to do that day, and sometimes her parents made her leave her phone in their room while she did her homework. Leigh also spent weekends with her family, so it was possible she was doing that. Just seeing this helped Janet feel better and detach from the thought that Leigh no longer liked her.

It's your turn to try and pick one or two thoughts that are getting you stuck and use one or both of these techniques to reframe your thought.

Thought: _____

_____

Advantages of Having this Thought	**Disadvantages of Having This Thought**
_____	_____
_____	_____
_____	_____
_____	_____

Thought: _____

_____

Challenging Old Beliefs with New Possibilities

Many of the thoughts that really get us stuck tend to be negative thoughts about ourselves. These thoughts make us believe we aren't worthy or that other people deserve good things more than we do. They can prevent us from speaking up, facing challenges, taking risks, and moving forward in pursuit of our values. Often at the core of these thoughts are some themes that may be creating these negative views. Some of these beliefs are:

- I'm unlovable.
- I'm not worthy of anything.
- I'm broken.
- I'm crazy.
- I'm inadequate or incompetent.
- I'm a failure at everything.
- I'm out of control.
- I'm weak.
- I'm undesirable or unattractive.
- I'm toxic or evil.

Adapted from Beck, Judith S. *Cognitive Behavior Therapy Basics and Beyond*. New York: The Guilford Press, 2011.

We now need to take a second look at some of the beliefs that often get us stuck, the ones that make us feel terrible about ourselves, instead of automatically taking them as truth. It can be difficult to do this when you are thinking about yourself, so in the following exercise we will use the perspective you have about a friend, or that a friend would have about you.

Pick one of the negative beliefs from the list on page 36, or another one along the same lines, that you have about yourself.

Write the belief here: _____

Now answer the following questions related to the belief:

Think of someone you know who you believe has the opposite trait. For example, if your thought is that you are unlovable or unworthy, think of someone who you believe to be lovable or worthy. Write their name here:

_____

What are some of the things they do that demonstrate these positive traits?

_____

_____

If your close friend or family member were having the same negative thoughts about themselves, what would you tell them?

_____

_____

What would your close friend or family member say you have done that is evidence that you have these positive traits (being lovable or worthy)?

_____

_____

Now list some behaviors you can practice to help demonstrate that you are the opposite of your belief. These are things you would do if you believed the opposite were true (that you were worthy or lovable). For example, if you thought you were unworthy, acting worthy might involve asking for things that you have earned, or practicing appearing confident with an upright posture and holding your head up high. If your belief is that you are crazy, some practices might be to talk more about your thoughts with others, try telling yourself that what you are thinking and feeling makes sense, or notice when others might be feeling the same way as you. You can use these behaviors in the next section.

_____

_____

_____

WRAP UP

In this section, you learned how to better understand your thoughts, how they are sticky, how they can trick you, and how to take a second look at the thoughts you take at face value. Here are the main takeaways:

- Thoughts can be very sticky, but with practice you can learn to choose whether you follow them or allow them to simply come and go.

- There are several types of common thinking mistakes that can trick you into believing your thoughts. Catching and labeling these mistakes allows you to pause before falling for the tricks. When you notice the mistake, you can create an alternative thought that is more accurate.

- You can check the facts on thoughts by becoming a scientist. Look at the thought as a hypothesis, then run an investigation to determine whether your thought has evidence to back it up. That allows you to create a more accurate thought based on the facts.

- Reframing thoughts is a way to change your perspective. Reframing gets you unstuck from your thought, decreases the emotional intensity the thought may have caused, helps you change unwanted behaviors related to the thought, and can free you from spending so much time focusing on one topic.

SECTION 3
YOUR BEHAVIORS

Behaviors is the second point on the CBT triangle. It involves how you act, what you do, how you spend your time, and how you react to situations. In this section you will learn that behaviors are separate from thoughts, and that having a thought does not have to lead to a behavior. You will learn how to take some of the values you chose in section 1 (see page 3) and set goals in line with those values. You will also learn how to stop doing behaviors you want to do less of and start doing positive alternative behaviors instead, and to consider behaviors you want to do more of. Finally, you will learn how to make an action plan to help you follow through on changing your behaviors and meeting your goals.

UNTANGLING THOUGHTS AND ACTIONS

Although thoughts and behaviors are connected on our CBT triangle, they are two separate points. However, we often believe that if we think a thought, not only is it based on fact, but it also actually has the power to make us do things—whether we want to or not. Our thoughts often result in a behavioral urge. Sometimes the urge is so strong or the behavior comes so quickly after a thought that there is no time between feeling the urge and doing the action. For example, you might have the urge to say something mean to your friend, and without even pausing or thinking, it just comes out of your mouth. Or you might have the thought, "No one wants to date me," and then when someone *does* ask you out, you say no because you think they are asking out of pity—all because of that thought. In short, your thoughts end up leading to urges and behaviors that then confirm to you that your thoughts were true.

Since thoughts and behaviors are different, we can actually choose how we *respond* to our thoughts. Having a thought, or even having an urge, doesn't need to automatically lead to an action. The following exercises will help you start untangling your thoughts, urges, and actions, and give you the freedom to make a different choice.

For this exercise, pick a thought that has resulted in an action you did not want. For example, thoughts such as "I hate myself," "I really want to eat this dessert," "He will never go out with me," "I don't want to go to school today," or "I'm ugly," could all result in different urges or actions. These might include punching a wall or avoiding social situations, eating something you later regret, not making eye contact with the person you like, pretending to be sick to stay home, or frowning throughout the day.

Pick a negative thought that has resulted in an action that you did not want:

_____

What do you notice or how do you feel when you have this thought?

_____

Now add the words "I'm having the thought that" in front of that thought, and write out the sentence:

_____

_____

What do you notice or how do you feel when you have this new thought?

_____

Now add "I'm noticing that I'm having the thought that" in front of the original thought:

_____

_____

What do you notice or how do you feel when you have this new thought?

_____

Now let's try this with an urge.

Write an urge you are having:

_____

Now add "I'm noticing that I'm having the urge to" in front of the urge:

_____

_____

How did you feel when thinking this way about an urge?

_____

Simply adding these phrases can help you step out of your automatic thinking style and start to see your thoughts just as thoughts, instead of believing they are true and acting on them. It can also put some distance between your urges and your actions. You can try this simple practice when you find yourself continuing to automatically act on urges.

Another way to start recognizing the separation between your thoughts and actions is to remember that a thought is just a bunch of letters that we form with sounds. We give our thoughts so much meaning that we forget they are just a string of sounds put together. Take the word "bowl." Set a timer for 30 seconds, then say "bowl" over and over until the timer goes off. What did you notice?

_____

When I do this, I tend to find that the sound of the "o" starts to sound weird. It stops sounding like a real word, and more like just a silly sound. It starts to take away the meaning of the word.

Now take one of the core negative beliefs you picked about yourself in section 2, and pick the key word (unworthy, unattractive, unlovable, etc.).

_____

Now set your timer for one minute, and keep saying that word out loud over and over until the timer goes off. What did you notice?

_____

_____

How is this different than how you usually respond to this word or thought?

_____

_____

Recognizing that some thoughts are just silly sounds can help you detach from the meaning of the word. This can give you the freedom to _choose_ to act however you want, which is not necessarily based on how your thoughts tell you to act. Try this exercise again the next time you find yourself having a thought that gives you an unhelpful urge.

GETTING WHERE YOU WANT TO GO

Changing behaviors is really hard, especially if you have been doing the same things over and over for a long time. You know you want to do things differently, but you can't help it. The first step is to identify the behaviors that you would like to change. What would you like to be doing more of? What do you want to do less of? What behaviors and actions end up causing you problems?

Go back and take a look at the values you prioritized from section 1 (see page 3). How would you say you are doing in living those values with your everyday actions? Are you acting in line with them the way you want to? How do your current behaviors fit with your values?

As you may remember, values are ideals or principles that guide us. They are the chosen life directions that you would like to follow. Values give our lives meaning. Once we know what our values are, we can then set goals to work on those values, which gives us something to build on and strive for. Values are also a way to bring purpose to the present moment, give us something to care about, and help us feel more connected to ourselves.

You can set specific smaller goals in line with values, or create what we call committed actions—a set of actions to create a life full of your wishes and hopes. If your values are your conscience guiding you on the journey, committed actions are the journey itself. Let's start figuring out your journey by creating specific goals in line with your values.

Write out the three to five values you identified in section 1, in order of importance:

_____

_____

_____

_____

_____

Pick the one that you want to start working on now.

_____

Let's use "be independent" as an example. The next step is to think about a concrete goal that supports this value. So if the value is being independent, a few goals might be getting an after-school job, doing your homework without your parents reminding you, doing your own laundry, getting a driver's license, or getting into college. What is your goal going to be?

_____

_____

Now let's think through all the steps that it will take to accomplish your goal. Let's say your goal was to get a job. You would have to break it down into smaller steps that might be (1) Googling options for local jobs, (2) picking out a few jobs you are interested in, (3) figuring out how you can apply to the jobs you want, (4) applying for the jobs, (5) interviewing for the jobs, (6) starting the job. And all of these can actually be broken down into even smaller steps. So now take your goal and break it down into 5–10 smaller steps.

_____

_____

_____

_____

_____

_____

_____

_____

Great work. Now that you have broken it down, what's the first step you will take?

_____

Adapted from Linehan, Marsha. *DBT® Skills Training Handouts and Worksheets*. New York: The Guilford Press, 2015.

As much as you want to follow through with the goal you set earlier, our intentions don't always end up resulting in the behaviors we plan. To make it more likely that you will follow through, let's think of some of the obstacles that could get in the way and some solutions to fix them. Sometimes the barriers to goals come from outside of you, like a person not giving you what you want, the weather not cooperating, a teacher not being flexible, or a random event. Other barriers come from within and include your own thoughts, emotions, and behaviors. For your own barriers, you can use some of the skills you are learning in this book to address them. Let's look at the example of getting a job and some of the possible barriers that might come up, as well as some solutions.

Step toward Goal	Possible Barriers	Solutions to Barriers
Googling options for jobs	Feeling overwhelmed, not knowing where to start	Asking a parent for help, talking to friends about how they approached their job search, trying out a few search terms
Picking a few potential jobs	Indecisiveness, uncertainty, negative thoughts about yourself	Using thought practices from section 2 to address negative thoughts
Finding out how to apply	Job postings don't have clear instructions, you can't find a place to submit an application, manager is not available	Sending an email to the contact person, going directly to the location of the office and asking questions, asking someone else working there how they applied
Applying	Lack of motivation, beliefs that you won't get the job	Using thought practices from section 2, committing to a friend that you will do it, planning a reward after you submit
Interviewing	Anxiety, negative beliefs	Using practices from the emotion section (see page 67), using thought practices from section 2
Starting	Fear, uncertainty	Creating a reward for the end of your first day, going to your first day as a test to see how it goes without committing

Now it's your turn. Write out the steps from your earlier goal and fill in the chart for possible barriers and solutions, using the previous chart as a guide.

Step toward Goal	Possible Barriers	Solutions to Barriers

HEALTHY BODY, HEALTHY MIND: EXERCISE

You probably know that exercise is good for you. Maybe you already exercise regularly because you are on a sports team. Maybe you visit the gym, go for runs, or you watch YouTube videos and do workouts at home. Or maybe you have a hard time getting moving.

Most teenagers should get an hour or more of exercise every day. Exercise has been shown to decrease depression, manage stress, increase positive emotions, and, of course, keep you physically healthy. By exercising regularly, you can deal with intense emotions more easily and stay calmer in tough situations.

Here are some tips to get the most benefits out of exercise:

- Try different types of exercise and find the one you either enjoy or mind the least. It's not nearly as important that you do a particular exercise, as it is that you do something you can tolerate. So, try out some new things with friends or by yourself to see what type of exercise is a good fit for you.

- Find ways to build exercise into your day, like taking the stairs instead of the elevator, taking walks after school, jogging down the street and back, or running in place while you are waiting.

- Find an exercise buddy. It's a lot easier to stick to a commitment if you have someone else to hold you accountable. So whether it's going to the gym, going for a run, doing a yoga video on YouTube together, or joining a soccer team, find a friend who also wants to get moving and commit to regular exercise.

WHAT ARE YOUR ALTERNATIVES?

In addition to setting goals related to your values, you may be thinking about particular behaviors that you would like to decrease or stop entirely. Many people want to yell less often, fight less with friends, stop sending texts on impulse, be late less often, stop binging or overeating, stop staying home all day, stop drinking or using drugs, or any number of behaviors. Think about three behaviors you might want to change and let's get some information about them.

EXERCISE: COLLECT YOUR OWN DATA

In order to better understand and start to notice the behaviors you want to change, it is helpful to collect data on when and how often you do them, which also helps you start noticing the urge before the behavior is completed. Over the next two days, use this sheet to track the three behaviors you want to change.

Behavior	Number	Times of Day	Place	With Who

When you were collecting this data, you may have realized that it was hard not to engage in these behaviors, or at least hard to know what else to do instead. This is because it is really hard to stop behaviors without having a *replacement* for that behavior. When you were younger, adults probably told you things like "No hitting, no running, no yelling." You might have known what you *were not* supposed to do, but not what you *were* supposed to do. It would have been helpful to have been told to keep your hands touching your sides instead of "no hitting." Or, instead of "no running," perhaps they could have told you to walk slowly. Instead of "no yelling," they could have told you to use a whisper. This replacement approach is what we are going to try with the behaviors you want to change.

Let's say you want to stop sending impulsive texts. What could you do instead? Perhaps you could make a rule that you have to write a draft of the text as a note and wait at least five minutes before sending. Or choose the people you are concerned about impulsively texting and make sure you run each text to them by a friend before sending. Or make a rule to wait at least ten minutes after reading a text before you respond. Adopting one of these behaviors makes it a lot easier to decrease impulsive texting. Let's write out up to three behaviors that you want to change now, and think of two possible alternative positive behaviors, or replacement behaviors. See the first line as an example.

Behavior to Decrease	Possible Replacement Behavior 1	Possible Replacement Behavior 2
Sending impulsive texts	Waiting ten minutes after reading a text to send a reply	Writing a draft of a text and waiting five minutes before sending

Now you have some ideas for what you can begin substituting for some of your unwanted behaviors. You may also already have some behaviors you know you want to increase, like exercising more often, eating healthier, getting up earlier, going out more, spending more time with your family, or others. What behaviors would you like to increase?

_____

_____

_____

_____

You may also think of some behaviors that you want to do, but that you avoid out of fear or anxiety. The way to change these behaviors is by gradually facing anxiety-provoking situations. For example, if you are anxious about giving presentations in front of the class, you might start by talking with one person about a topic. Then, you might talk about a topic in front of a few of your friends. You could also practice giving a presentation while you are just hanging out with friends or family in a more informal setting. The more you practice giving presentations, the easier it will be to do them in real life.

Consider some behaviors or situations that you avoid doing because they make you anxious. Avoiding them long term may go against the values you have, so it may be important to face these fears. If any behaviors apply, add them to your list below.

_____

_____

_____

_____

Now comes the hard part: getting yourself to actually do these behaviors. The principles of changing behaviors are actually pretty simple. *Positive reinforcement* is when something rewarding happens that increases the chance that you will do the behavior again. Think about your teachers. Who would you work harder for: the teacher who gives you extra credit for participation (positive reinforcement), or the teacher who brings your grade down for not participating? Most people prefer the extra credit version. We are motivated by rewards, not punishments. Think of the reasons you do things. You study to get a good grade, you help your friends because they appreciate you, you do your chores to please your parents and perhaps get their praise.

Sometimes we need to find ways to reward ourselves for behaviors that take effort—to create our own positive reinforcement. These rewards could be listening to your favorite song, treating yourself to your favorite beverage from the coffee shop, talking to your friend on the phone, playing a game you enjoy, getting time to relax, watching an episode of your favorite show, or any number of other motivators. Let's brainstorm some rewards that might work for you.

List out some rewards you can create for yourself. If you find yourself getting stuck, think about the things you enjoy doing most.

_____

_____

_____

_____

_____

_____

_____

_____

In addition to rewards, making a commitment to other people can be very helpful for following through on something. These should be people you trust who will hold you to your commitment and can celebrate with you when you accomplish your goal. Who are some of those people?

_____

_____

YOUR ACTION PLAN

Now that we've laid the foundation for changing your behaviors and working on goals, let's create a plan that helps you follow through. This plan should feel challenging but doable—not overwhelming. The best way to start is to focus on a small section of behaviors and goals. Whatever you choose, it's important to phrase the behaviors for what you *will* do (rather than what you won't), so you stay motivated and are clear on what needs to happen.

Let's go back to the value you chose as your priority to work on now (see page 47). Now look at the behaviors that you want to decrease, increase, or stop avoiding because of anxiety. Of all of these behaviors, are there any that are related to the value that you chose? For example, if your value was to be a good friend, a behavior to change in line with this value might be to stop impulsively texting because it has caused fights with some friends. In this case, the positive behavior you are adding is waiting five minutes before responding to any text. Or, if your value was to lead others and you get anxious talking in front of people or being in groups, you might want to work on facing your anxiety in these situations. Your behavior could then be to practice going to parties and group events. Perhaps your value is living a healthy lifestyle, so you might want to work on trying to exercise several times a week. Let's take some time now to put together your committed action plan based on the value you want to work on first.

Priority value: _____

Goal you already set related to this value:

_____

New behaviors to work on in line with this value (these could be your new alternative behaviors, behaviors to increase, or behaviors related to anxiety):

- _____

- _____

- _____

To make it easier for you to practice these new behaviors, it helps to turn them into concrete, specific goals. We will set goals for one week at a time. For example, if the behavior you are adding is exercising, you might set the goal of going to the gym two times this week. Or if you are going to wait five minutes before texting people back, you might give yourself the goal of doing this three times a day for a week. If you are working on spending time in bigger groups, you might set the goal of finding one or two group activities to do this week. Go ahead and make very specific weekly goals for the three behaviors so that you will be able to say easily if you accomplished them or not.

Goals this week:

- Behavior 1:

  _____

- Behavior 2:

  _____

- Behavior 3:

  _____

Great! Now, go back to the goal you initially set related to this value (see page 47). Let's pick the first two steps. In my example of getting a job, those are (1) Googling local options for jobs, and (2) considering these options. Therefore, the goal would be to find time to do those two steps sometime in the next week, and we would add that to our list.

Value goals:

- _____

- _____

You now have five goals to work on this week: three goals related to behaviors you want to change, and two smaller steps in line with a bigger goal. Now we need to commit to a day and time to work on each of these goals and create rewards for each. Take a look at this example first, and then try creating your own.

Week Of: *September 2*

Value: *Being Independent*

Goal	Time, Day/Date I Plan to Do This	Person Holding Me Accountable	Reward I Get
Googling local options for jobs	Friday when I get home from school at 4:30 p.m.	My friend Danielle	My favorite dinner
Considering job options	Sunday at noon	My friend Danielle	Starbucks
Doing homework as soon as I am home three times this week	Monday, Tuesday, Thursday	Dad	Talking to friends on my phone as soon as homework is done
Being on time for school two times this week	Tuesday, Thursday	Mom	Listening to my favorite music while I wait for homeroom to start
Going somewhere by myself once this week	Saturday	My friend Joanne	Sleepover with Joanne

Now it's your turn. Fill out your weekly committed action plan for this week:

Week Of: _____

Value: _____

Goal	Time, Day/Date I Plan to Do This	Person Holding Me Accountable	Reward I Get

Come back to this section after week one!

So: how did it go? What barriers came up when you tried to accomplish these goals? We may need to think through ways to solve some of these barriers.

Fill in this chart if you had any barriers that got in the way of your goals.

Goal	Barriers	Possible Solution to Barriers

Now, it's time to try again for the next week. Add back in any goals you did not accomplish and try implementing some of the solutions you came up with for the barriers. You can also try a more appealing reward if the one you picked was not motivating enough. If you accomplished your steps related to the larger goal, go ahead and pick the next one or two steps toward that bigger goal. For the behaviors you worked on, you could increase the number of times per week you do the behavior for continued practice, or if the behavior is something you are sure you can continue on your own, you can swap in a new one. Here is an example for week two. Anything in bold is new or adjusted from the original.

Week Of: *September 10*

Value: *Being Independent*

Goal	Time, Day/Date I Plan to Do This	Person Holding Me Accountable	Reward I Get
Finding how to apply to jobs I want	**Wednesday at 5:00 p.m.**	**Mom**	**Ice cream after dinner**
Applying	**Saturday at 2:00 p.m.**	**My friend John**	**Go out to dinner**
Doing homework as soon as I am home four times this week	Monday, Tuesday, Wednesday, Thursday	Dad	Talking to friends on my phone as soon as homework is done
Being on time for school three times this week	Monday, Tuesday, Thursday	Mom	Listening to my favorite music while I wait for homeroom to start
Going somewhere by myself once this week	Friday	My friend Joanne	Go shopping with Joanne

Now it's your turn again. Take some time to fill out your weekly committed action plan for week two.

Week Of: _____

Value: _____

Goal	Time, Day/Date I Plan to Do This	Person Holding Me Accountable	Reward I Get

After you are done, do the same evaluation and adjustment process again, and reset goals for the following week. You can follow this process at the end of every week. As time goes on, you will be able to add in more behaviors and goals, or maybe shift and prioritize a whole different value.

Remember that your committed actions are the journey, so they are always continuing and changing. The more you can implement this weekly, the more you will be living the life you want and becoming the person you would like to be. This process is not easy and takes practice, patience, and perseverance. But if you stick to it and keep working, continuing to find rewards that motivate you, you will observe your behaviors changing and find that you're accomplishing your larger goals.

WRAP UP

This section focused on how to change behaviors that are unhelpful, how to start adding in or increasing behaviors you want to do, and how to do a better job of living your life in line with your values. The main takeaways are:

- It's possible to separate your thoughts and urges from your behaviors. Just because you think a thought or have an urge does not automatically mean you have to act on it.

- It's important to figure out what you want to change based on the values you want to live by.

- Once you know some behaviors that you want to change or stop, it helps to change them into alternative positive behaviors so that you know what to do instead of what *not* to do.

- Thinking ahead about possible barriers to accomplishing goals is an important step, so you can problem solve and be ready for them.

- Rewarding yourself for your hard work is a vital part of changing behaviors and accomplishing challenging goals.

- Once you create your weekly plan for committed actions, it is important to evaluate where you need to problem solve, repeat goals, and make new ones for the following week.

- Your committed actions are the journey.

SECTION 4
YOUR EMOTIONS

Here, we'll discuss the third point on the CBT triangle: emotions. In this section you will learn to manage difficult emotions—such as anger, sadness and depression, and anxiety—that could be contributing to negative thoughts or holding you back from your goals. You'll learn how to accept these challenging and intense emotions and move forward from them. Specifically, we will review techniques for managing anger and understanding what might be underneath your anger, how to manage sadness and depression, and how to get moving when you feel frozen in place from these emotions. We also look at techniques for managing anxiety, including how to learn to control it instead of letting it control you, and how to avoid avoiding.

WORKING WITH DIFFICULT EMOTIONS

It's normal to wish you didn't have to feel intense emotions. They can be really painful and hard to sit with. Unfortunately, avoiding inevitable painful emotions is not good for anyone. Think about emotions as waves. When you are at the beach, and you see a big wave coming, what are your options? You can run from it, fight it, or ride it. If you run from it, it likely will catch you eventually. If you try to fight it, you might get dragged down under the water. But if you ride it, it can take you to shore. That's how to best handle emotions. Just like waves, they have the power to catch up to us if we run from them, or drag us down if we fight them. So ride them out instead.

This might sound incredibly hard. But here's a fact that may help: Most emotions only last about 90 seconds. That probably sounds very short to you because you might continue to feel an emotion for a long time. However, the reason most people feel emotions over long periods of time is because we have a tendency to keep feeding them, or reinforcing them. If we allowed the burst of emotion to come and go without thinking about the problem that caused the emotion or why we feel the way we do, the emotion would actually come and go pretty quickly. For example, have you ever stepped out into the street and then realized a car was coming? You probably felt fear and stepped back. If you thought, "Phew, that was close," and then let it go, after a minute or two you probably didn't feel fear anymore. However, if you spent the rest of the day thinking about how you almost got hit by a car, you would perpetuate the emotion and continue to feel the fear.

The best way to allow emotions to come and go is by accepting them. When I use the word "acceptance," I *do not* mean agreement. We don't have to agree with, like, want, or be on board with our emotions. But we do have to acknowledge that they exist, that any given emotion is how you feel at any point in time. When you don't accept that you are having an emotion, you might fight it and make it worse, or push it away—which will result in it coming up later in ways you don't want. By denying it, fighting it, or pretending it is something else, we are creating unnecessary suffering for ourselves. But if we see emotions for what they are, we can cultivate the capacity for "normal" emotional pain along with the ability to move forward with minimal suffering.

Let's think about how this fits into the big picture. If you accepted your emotions, what would that mean? What would you need to then do in order to meet your goals? How would you need to take care of yourself? Being accepting of emotions might mean pausing and taking several deep breaths. It could mean taking a break from a conversation and going into the bathroom. It could mean going for a walk. It might mean writing in a journal. It's important to think about the steps you want to take during the time you are feeling the intense emotion so the emotion doesn't get in the way of your goals or values.

Taking these steps gives you the opportunity to make a choice on how you want to act in response to your emotions. As we discussed in the last section, you don't need to automatically act on every urge that a thought, or in this case an emotion, causes. You can give yourself the opportunity to make a choice that you believe is going to help you achieve your long-term goals, rather than acting without thinking.

Certain emotions may get you stuck more often than others. We will discuss how to manage anger, sadness and depression, and anxiety specifically.

Anger

If you are like most teenagers, you feel angry (or at least irritable!) quite often. It can be frustrating being in this stage of your life. Your parents still want you to follow their rules, ask you to do homework when you don't want to, make you do chores, force you to participate in family activities when you don't want to, and won't let you do some of the things that your friends are allowed to do. You also might get angry at teachers for making you do so much schoolwork, or for embarrassing you in front of the class. Your friends might make you angry when they gossip about you or others, or you might feel angry with the person you're dating if they do things you don't like.

As common as anger is, it can also get the best of us. Sometimes it hijacks our plans, and we end up acting on a behavior that we wish we hadn't. For example, someone might end up sending a ranting angry text or post something on social media out of anger and later they wished they hadn't. Or, anger may lead some people to curse or yell, which might get them in trouble at home or school. Some people break up with a sweetheart out of anger, and then wish they hadn't. Others turn to alcohol or drugs to try to block out the anger, which often leads to other types of problems. We want to be able to manage our anger instead of letting it carry us away. Here are two exercises that can help you manage your anger effectively.

A technique called progressive muscle relaxation can help you relax and let go of tension when you are feeling angry. The idea is to tighten and hold small muscle groups for a few seconds, and then release them for double that time to really feel the relief, and let the anger recede as you do this. If it is helpful, as you do this you can imagine the anger melting away every time you release, or else just focus on the sensation when you stop tightening and release.

Start with your head. Scrunch your face together for five seconds, and then let it go for ten. Move your chin down toward your neck to stretch your neck for five seconds, then release for ten. Shrug your shoulders all the way up to your ears and hold for five seconds, then release for ten. Make a bicep with your upper arms for five seconds, then release for ten. Squeeze your hands like you are squeezing a lemon for five seconds, then release for ten. Stretch out your legs off the ground and flex your feet for five seconds, then release for ten. Scrunch your toes in your shoe like a fist for five seconds, then release for ten.

You may want to do this a second time, double the amount of time you hold/release, or break up the muscle groups into even smaller groups. Experiment and see what works best.

Observe how you feel after this exercise. Can you feel how the physical experience of your anger has released? Has the emotion become less intense in your body?

EXERCISE: RELEASING ANGER MENTALLY

Anger can lead to thoughts or urges within you that you just need to get out. You may be tempted to get them out by yelling at someone, telling them how much they have hurt you, telling them how much you are suffering, or trying to get revenge. However, these tactics could really interfere with your goals and probably act against your values.

One way to release these strong feelings of anger without doing damage is to write them down in a letter that you never give the person. You can write out what you want to say and all the reasons you are angry. Don't hold back! This will provide a sense of release and relief. Then throw the letter away, lock it in a drawer, password protect it, or let it go in some other way. See how you feel after you write out all the emotion without acting on your urges.

_____

_____

_____

_____

_____

_____

EXERCISE: SELF-COMPASSION MEDITATION

Another way to help manage anger in the moment is to send yourself compassion. There are many ways to do this, but for this exercise, you will focus on sending four wishes to yourself. Set a timer for three minutes, and then repeat the following out loud or in your head until the timer goes off: "*May I be happy, may I be healthy, may I be loved, and may I live with ease.*" Over the course of the meditation, observe what thoughts, emotions, urges, or any other experiences come up for you—then let them go. As you express compassion for yourself during these hard moments and feelings, you may notice the anger start to dissipate and your body and mind relax.

WHAT'S UNDERNEATH YOUR ANGER?

If you experience anger often, it is possible that anger is actually an easier emotion for you to experience than some other emotions that might be underneath it. You might actually feel sadness, but anger comes more easily because you can blame someone or something for your emotions. Or you might feel shame at something you did or said, but that immediately turns to anger, which takes the focus off your own actions. In order to figure out whether your anger is actually the main emotion or a secondary emotion, it can be helpful to think about what typically makes you feel angry.

EXERCISE: WHAT'S UNDERNEATH YOUR ANGER?

Below, spend a few minutes writing about the things that usually make you angry. See if there might be some alternative causes to your anger besides not getting what you want. If these emotions are sadness or fear, you can use some of the exercises in the following sections to help manage them.

The last thing I got angry about was _____.

I was angry because _____.

I usually get angry (at who) _____

(in what situations) _____

(time of day) _____

(when I think about) _____.

Possible other emotions that could be underneath my anger are:

_____

_____

_____

HEALTHY BODY, HEALTHY MIND: SLEEP

You've probably been told most of your life that sleep is vital to feeling good, being in a good mood, and doing your best in school and activities. Maybe you have firsthand experience with what it feels like when you don't get enough sleep because you were up way too late talking with friends, doing homework, or watching YouTube videos. You probably felt irritable, had no energy, had trouble concentrating, and just felt out of it. We all *need* sleep in order to function.

You might think that you can function just fine on five to six hours of sleep (or less), but the recommendation for teens is eight to ten hours of sleep a night for optimal functioning. If you're *not* getting eight to ten hours for whatever reason, know that you could be functioning much better, your mood could be more balanced, your emotions less intense, and your reactions less impulsive.

Here are some tips for getting more balanced sleep:

- Try to go to bed at the same time every night, and wake up at the same time every morning—even on the weekends. Although you may love sleeping in on the weekends, it makes it much harder to fall asleep early enough during the week and wake up feeling refreshed for school.

- Keep your room cool. It is much better for sleep to have slightly cooler temperatures than warmer. Make sure you have comfortable blankets and sheets, as feeling uncomfortable throughout the night leads to tossing and turning.

- Create a sleep routine before you go to bed. This could include ways to wind down from the day like a hot shower, deep breathing, reading a book (not on your phone!), putting your phone away 30 minutes before bed, listening to calming music, listening to a podcast, or dimming the lights. Do this routine every night.

Sadness and Depression

Feeling sad, down, or depressed at times is a normal part of being a teenager. Life is hard, unfair, disappointing, and many times it isn't what we hoped it would be. As we've learned, taking some time to acknowledge your emotions and allow yourself to feel sadness is important. However, if you find that you are spending a lot of time dwelling in sadness or depression, withdrawing from friends and family, eating or sleeping less often, and not able to concentrate in school, you may need to do some work on managing these emotions. This workbook can help you get out of feelings of depression. However, if the depression is persistent and you are having a hard time doing it on your own, make sure you talk to someone you trust for help.

On a more serious level, for some people, depression can lead to thoughts about suicide, self-harm behaviors, or beliefs that life is not worth living. If you are having these thoughts or urges, it is *very* important to talk to someone. The National Suicide Hotline is available 24 hours, 7 days a week either by phone or by online chat. You can call them at **1-800-273-8255** or talk through an online chat, or reach out to your parents or school counselor. If you would prefer to talk with an organization specifically geared toward the unique needs of LGBTQ teens, contact the Trevor Project's hotline at **1-888-488-7386**. They are also available around the clock.

Every emotion has an urge, and for sadness the typical urge is to withdraw. This means not doing the activities that you usually enjoy, not seeing friends and family as often, not feeling motivated to do schoolwork or participate in activities, or not having your usual energy level. When this strikes, a lot of people think they should just wait until their motivation comes back and they feel ready to engage in life again. However, depression doesn't work that way.

The truth is that we need to push ourselves to do things, and then we get the motivation. If you know any runners, they will likely tell you that sometimes they struggle with the motivation to go for a run. But after the first mile or two, they become more motivated to keep running. Most activities are like that with depression. Get going, and the motivation follows. For example, you may have a hard time getting out of bed in the morning, and the idea of going to school feels overwhelming. So, the first step would be to sit up in bed, or perhaps get out of bed. Maybe the next step is to take a shower or get dressed. Or perhaps you have to write a paper and you just don't know where to start and don't want to do it. Here, the first step would be to sit down and open your computer. Then open a blank document. Perhaps write your name and the date. Although each step takes effort, once you start doing one step, it gets a little easier to do the next step.

Easier said than done, though, right? Try the two exercises on the following pages to start taking some steps. The first is designed to help you get your sadness to a more manageable level when it feels extreme, and the second to help you get moving when your motivation is low or nonexistent.

EXERCISE: WHEN YOUR SADNESS FEELS TOO DEEP

As we discussed earlier, emotions are like waves. If you fight the emotion or run away, it will drag you down. If you let it engulf you, it might swallow you whole. Instead, the goal is to ride the emotional wave. To do this, you need to use mindfulness to observe your emotions. Try this exercise with your sadness.

Pay attention to your emotion as though you are an observer not attached to the experience. How does sadness feel in your body? How do you know you are sad? Do you feel something in your throat? In your chest? In your head? In your stomach? What is the energy like in your body? Do you feel the urge to cry? Any other urges? How long are these sensations lasting? Are they changing in strength or staying consistent? What else do you notice about your emotion? When was the last time you felt this way? How long did it last? Try acknowledging that this emotion is here right now. Whatever it is, it's already here. Nothing to do, nothing to change, just notice how things are in this moment. Remember that things are always changing, that things will be different in the next moment, and this is just how this moment feels.

Take some time to reflect after that exercise. What did you notice?

_____

Is this similar or different to how you usually respond to your sadness?

_____

Often, when people have an extreme emotion, it is hard to remember that you might feel different, that you have ever felt different, or that sadness is just one emotion you have. Sometimes we make it seem like there is no other option but to dwell in an emotion or to get stuck in it, and declare it our worst enemy. But the reality is that you can treat it like a toothache, a stubbed toe, a feeling of excitement, the sound of a song you like, or any other experience. It's not more or less important, it is just one of many. Taking a step back like this to observe the sadness can help us get some distance from it and not feel like it defines us or has full control.

Adapted from Segal, Zindel V., J. Mark, G. Williams, and John D. Teasdale. *Mindfulness-Based Cognitive Therapy for Depression*. New York: The Guilford Press, 2013.

The best thing you can do to help your depression is to get active and do something physical to get your energy up and yourself moving. Try some of these when you are feeling down. Then use the following chart to make some notes and gather information for how each of these helped your mood.

- **Jumping jacks.** Do jumping jacks for a minute to get moving. Once you do these, you may find that you have more energy to participate in your day.
- **Stand with an upright posture.** Hold your head high, look up not down, don't slouch or hunch, and spread your arms and hands out as though you are open to whatever is happening in the moment. Observe how your mood shifts.
- **Dance.** Put on your favorite upbeat song and break it down. Pick a beat you can't resist.
- **Run in place.** Or jog around your room or around your house.
- **Jump rope.** Keep a jump rope with you so when you need a little boost you can whip it out and jump.

Activity Type	Depression Before (0 to 10)	Depression After (0 to 10)	Notes on Experience

Anxiety

Anxiety. Just seeing that word might make you feel some tension. Anxiety really likes to be the boss of you. It likes to call the shots and dictate what you can and can't do. It gets in the way of your sleep, might interfere with your eating, could interrupt your fun activities, and might not let you stop thinking about something. It is really powerful. It can run your life and prevent you from doing things you enjoy if you let it. Most people have some worries and concerns, but it becomes a bigger problem when you are only living your life based on what your anxiety tells you.

Similar to depression and sadness, anxiety and fear also have an associated urge: usually avoidance. Think about anxiety like a bad guard dog. A good guard dog is supposed to bark when there is danger. However, when you have anxiety, your mind and body "barks" at many things, whether they are dangerous or not. So it is important to teach your mind and body what is dangerous and what is not by allowing yourself to practice being in challenging situations and facing your fears. It may help to take stock of what you are regularly avoiding or what your mind is telling you could be a threatening or dangerous situation.

Let's examine how much anxiety gets in the way of your life. Check off any of the following activities that you avoid due to fear, worry, or anxiety.

☐ Making phone calls

☐ Going out with friends

☐ Eating in public

☐ Talking to adults

☐ Performing in front of others

☐ Going to a party

☐ Doing group projects

☐ Meeting new people

☐ Flying on a plane

☐ Going to a public bathroom

☐ Walking into class late

☐ Being the center of attention

☐ Taking a test

☐ Disagreeing with someone

☐ Making direct eye contact

☐ Going on a date

☐ Asking someone out

☐ Buying something at a store

☐ Being in crowds

☐ Going to the movies alone

☐ Being seen with your parents

☐ Running into people you know

☐ Asking someone for help

☐ Playing on a sports team

If you checked many items, it's likely that anxiety has been controlling you. Let's think about how you can take back control. To manage anxiety it is helpful to address underlying thoughts and behaviors.

EXERCISE: GETTING TO THE BOTTOM OF ANXIETY

Similar to what we did in section 2, you can figure out what thoughts are preventing you from living life the way you want to. Look at the example answer in italics, and then answer the following questions for yourself:

What situation are you worried about and what are your worries? *I am worried about walking into class late because I believe everyone will stare at me and judge me.*

If this were true, what would that mean to you? *That people are laughing at me and making fun of me.*

And if that were the case, what would that mean to you? *That I am the butt of everyone's jokes.*

And if that were true, what would that mean about you? *That I am a failure at everything.*

Okay, now it's your turn.

What situation are you worried about and what are your worries?

_____

If this were true, what would that mean to you?

_____

 And if that were the case, what would that mean to you?

_____

And if that were true, what would that mean about you?

_____

Remember our core belief practice in section 2? Often these anxious thoughts are linked to one of those core beliefs. Before moving forward, go back to page 37 and try the exercise about core beliefs.

Adapted from Beck, Judith S. *Cognitive Behavior Therapy Basics and Beyond.* New York: The Guilford Press, 2011.

Now that we have addressed some of the thoughts that might be associated with your anxiety, we need to address the urge to avoid. Luckily, we already have the tools to do this from our behavior section and just need to put them in place here. Remember the committed action practices in section 3 (page 58)? With anxiety, we want to practice facing our fears as a committed action. Go back to the list of situations you avoid because of anxiety. Pick one to start practicing with.

Here's an example.

Situation to practice facing: *Walking into class late*

Now, we need to come up with some smaller, more manageable steps to work toward fully being in this situation, just like the steps we thought through in section 3. If we broke our example down, it might look like this:

1. Get to class five minutes early.

2. Get to class one minute early.

3. Walk into class right as the bell rings.

4. Walk into class right after the bell rings.

5. Walk into class seconds after the bell rings.

6. Walk into class one minute after the bell rings.

7. Walk into class three minutes late.

8. Walk into class five minutes late.

Try coming up with your own list by breaking it down into manageable steps.

Situation to practice facing: _____

_____

Small steps toward the larger goal:

1. _____

2. _____

3. _____

4. _____

5. _____

6. _____

7. _____

8. _____

9. _____

10. _____

Now, try the steps out. Each time you try a step, it helps to keep some data. Rate your anxiety before, during, and after from 0 (no anxiety) to 10 (highest anxiety). Use the following sheet to track your progress.

Step	Anxiety Before (0 to 10)	Anxiety During (0 to 10)	Anxiety After (0 to 10)	Notes on Experience

Perhaps pick some small rewards you can give yourself for each step and a bigger reward for your last step. It sometimes can seem overwhelming in the beginning, but as you make your way through, you may find you were able to tolerate the anxiety better than you imagined you would.

WRAP UP

In this section we discussed emotions, and the importance of allowing them to be there without pushing them away or fighting them. We also dove deeper into anger, depression, and anxiety and discussed exercises to better manage them. Here are the main takeaways.

- We cannot prevent feeling emotions. When you feel difficult emotions, it is important to acknowledge them and allow them to come and go so they don't drag you down.

- Anger is a powerful emotion that can result in acting on behaviors we regret. You can release anger physically or mentally. It is also important to look under the anger to see if another emotion is behind it.

- Feeling down or sad is normal as a teenager, but feeling withdrawn or isolated can get in the way of your goals. Getting active and throwing yourself into activities can really help improve motivation and fight depression.

- Anxiety likes to control your behavior, but using techniques to manage your thoughts and face challenging situations can give you back control.

SECTION 5
PUTTING YOUR TOOLS TO WORK

Now that you have learned how to work on the three points of the CBT triangle, we are going to discuss how you can apply these strategies to different parts of your life. We will look at ways to use these skills at home with parents, with siblings, and on your own. We will also address strategies you can use at school for managing the pressure of grades, working on your behavior with teachers and in classes, and calming your body down when you feel too much pressure. You will learn ways to use skills with friends or in dating relationships when you have negative thoughts that get you stuck, when you are having a tough conversation and don't know what to say, and when anxiety gets in your way. We will go over some strategies we have already discussed as well as some new ones you can use in these situations.

AT HOME

No one has the perfect parents or the perfect family. As a teen, you may constantly struggle with trying to become more independent while still living with your parents under their roof and following their rules. You might get into arguments with them about your curfew, when to do homework, how much you can be on your phone, or if you can even have a phone at all. You might have a hard time getting along with your siblings or feel like your parents favor them. You might feel like the black sheep in your family when it comes to feeling emotions, especially if your family members don't understand your emotions. Whatever your situation is, home life can be challenging. Here are some exercises to help.

EXERCISE: FINDING A HAPPY MEDIUM

I know it is really hard to be at this age and stage. Try to remember (if you can) that it is also surprisingly hard to be a parent of a teen and figure out the best way to keep your child safe, healthy, and happy. One of the biggest challenges that often comes up during the teenage years is when you want to do something and your parent(s) will not let you—for example, having a later curfew, or spending time alone with someone you really like.

For this exercise, let's use the curfew example. Place yourself on the following scale where you believe your curfew should be, and where your parent or parents think it should be. One end of the spectrum is not being allowed out at all; the other end is not having a curfew and being allowed to do whatever you want. Draw a line where you believe you should be. Now draw a line representing where your parents tell you to be.

| Never allowed out | Out during the day | In before dinner | 7:00 p.m. | 10:00 p.m. | Can stay out as late as desired |

Your goal now is to talk to them about trying to get a little closer to the middle of your line and their line. This is a helpful way to practice negotiating and compromising. If you want an 11:00 p.m. curfew and they want you in every day by dinnertime, you won't get anywhere if you just insist on an 11:00 p.m. curfew. Try asking for an 8:00 p.m. curfew instead. Your parents may be willing to work with you or may not be, but they will be more likely to listen to you and consider a slight increase than they will a complete change. What's a reasonable goal for your curfew?

Now let's think of two other areas of conflict where you and your parents disagree on privileges. Complete the following chart with markers for where you and your parents are. Then establish the middle point, and set a new goal to talk to them about it.

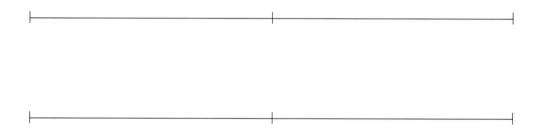

Siblings

In section 3, we discussed how to reinforce and reward yourself for doing something challenging. You can use the same approach to reinforce your siblings when they do behaviors you actually want them to do. For example, does a sibling often take your stuff without asking? Using reinforcement, you can get them to ask before they borrow something. Every time they actually do ask before taking something (even if it doesn't happen very often), reinforce it. If you have a younger sibling, you can give them stickers or small items to reward them. If they are closer to your age, you can thank them, tell them you appreciate what they're doing, or give them something they want, like music, a turn sitting in the front seat in the car or choosing what to watch on TV, or something else that is important to them.

EXERCISE: REINFORCING SIBLINGS

Let's list three behaviors that you would like your siblings to do. Remember, if it is a behavior you would like them to *stop* doing, phrase it as an alternative behavior to increase instead of an admonishment, such as "Please ask before you borrow something," instead of "Never take my stuff without asking."

_____

_____

_____

Now let's think about what rewards you could give them for each behavior.

_____

_____

_____

Now go ahead and try it. The key is to do it a few times for each behavior so they learn that when they do a behavior you want to see they will get a reward. Over time, you can start decreasing the amount of times you reinforce them, but for a while it is important to be consistent so they know they will get something rewarding each time they do it. Otherwise they will just go back to doing the behavior you didn't want.

Your Room

Do you spend a lot of time in your room? There could be many reasons for that. Maybe you don't enjoy spending time with your family. Maybe you are feeling sad or depressed and don't feel like getting out of bed. Or maybe you just love your room and feel safer and more comfortable in there. Whatever the reason, if you spend a lot of time in your room, it can be a place to help your mood and emotions improve. What types of decorations do you have in your room? What memories are on display? Whatever your room looks like, you can always improve it and create an inviting space that helps you manage challenging emotions. The idea is to create a specific distress tolerance space, which is a place you can go to get some distance from a problem, take the edge off, or think more positively.

EXERCISE: CREATE YOUR DISTRESS TOLERANCE SPACE

First, designate a place in your room for this. If you don't have your own room, find a small space somewhere in the place you live. You may be tempted to use your bed, but that can get confusing when you try to tell your body to sleep and it thinks your bed is a place for you to be awake and active. What's a good comfy spot that is not your bed? It could be your desk, a chair, the floor right next to your bed, or another space in your home. You can be honest about your needs with your family or anyone else you live with—show them the space and tell them that it's the place you go when you're feeling distressed.

Where will your space be?

_____

Now let's make a list of items to have ready or keep in this space. Think of the things you use to feel better or when you need a mental break. Some examples include watching a funny YouTube video, lighting scented candles, incense, or a diffuser, listening to calming music, doing a puzzle, playing with your pet, wrapping yourself in a comfortable sweater or blanket, drinking something soothing like tea or hot chocolate, looking at photos of your friends or a place you enjoyed, meditating, or playing with a fidget cube, modeling clay, or putty. Below, list some possible items you can use and activities you can set up in your space.

- _____
- _____
- _____
- _____
- _____
- _____
- _____
- _____
- _____
- _____

Great! Now spend some time putting some of them out and making them easily accessible. This way, as soon as you need them they are there for you, and you won't have to think about what you can do or spend time setting things up. The next time a difficult emotion arises at home, head to your space and reach for your tools. Notice how you're able to soothe yourself in this way.

Adapted from Rathus, Jill H., and Alec L. Miller. *DBT Skills Manual for Adolescents*. New York: The Guilford Press, 2014.

AT SCHOOL

School is the place that you spend the most time besides home, so it's really important to figure out how to feel okay being there. If you are like most teenagers, there are days (maybe many days) when you don't want to go to school and would prefer to stay home. Maybe you don't really enjoy school, are having a hard time keeping your grades up, think your teachers are too mean or strict, or you feel generally stressed by the pressure and competition. This is totally normal. But at the same time, you need to go to school. You don't have a choice. So the best thing to do is to find a way to manage school while you're there.

Grades

Let's start with your grades. Everyone does differently in school, and you may have found that some subjects come easily to you and some are much harder. Or maybe you generally have a hard time in school across all of your subjects. It could be that you do well in school, but you feel a lot of pressure to keep living up to expectations. Sometimes you may feel like how you do in school defines who you are as a person. This type of thinking is a problem for many reasons.

EXERCISE: WHAT MAKES ME, ME?

Let's address the problem of school feeling like it's your entire identity, and the thought that if you are not a good student, you may as well be nothing. Remember the pie chart we did in section 2 (see page 34)? We are going to do something similar here. Think about who you are and what you enjoy. This could include your hobbies, sports teams, being a member of your family, an organization or community you belong to, being a good friend, your religious faith, or many other things. Write out some of the things that are part of who you are here.

_____

_____

_____

Look at the different slices of the following pie chart below. Fill in school/grades, as well as some of these other aspects of yourself in the even slices.

Now take a look at your chart. Notice that school and grades is just a small percentage of what makes you, you. Whether your grades are something you are proud of or something you struggle with, your grades are only one part of your whole person. This is important to remember when you start to feel pressure to do well in school, either because you need to live up to what you already have done, or whether you are trying to do better. When your self-esteem starts to crumble based on your performance at school, remember this chart. Grades are only one part of you! Take a picture of this chart to remind you that your grades are not everything important about you.

Teachers

Teachers may present you with another challenge. Maybe you don't get along with them or disagree with them, perhaps you believe they don't like you, or you just plain don't respect them. Whatever the case is, it is important to be able to get through the day with the teachers you have. Think back to our section on changing your behavior (see page 41). What goals do you have related to the classroom? It could be to pass your classes, not get detention, or not interrupt someone else. Are there goals you can set for behaviors to increase, or positive alternative behaviors to things you would like to stop doing in the classroom?

EXERCISE: SETTING GOALS FOR BEING IN CLASS

When it comes to interacting with your teachers or thinking about your behavior in your classes, what are some behaviors you would like to increase? Some ideas might be raising your hand more frequently to answer questions, giving your teachers more compliments, tightening your mouth shut when you have the urge to talk back, taking deep breaths to stay calm in difficult classes, practicing speaking in front of the class more often, or only speaking when you have something nice to say.

List out three behaviors that you plan to work on improving in classes and with your teachers. Remember to write out the specific goal for the week, barriers, solution to barriers, and the reward you will give yourself, just like we did in section 3. You can use the example at the top as a guide.

Weekly Goal	Possible Barriers	Solutions to Barriers	Reward
Raise hand once a day in class this week	Anxiety, not knowing the answer	Do deep breathing, study ahead of time	Listen to a good song after class

Dealing with Pressure

Pressure can make school really challenging. You might be in a school where everyone is competitive about grades. You may be preparing to take a standardized test like the SAT or ACT, or are in the midst of college applications. You might feel like you're drowning in all your classes, trying to gear up for exams, getting pressure from your parents, or putting pressure on yourself. Any of these pressures can lead to stress and feeling overwhelmed. When we talked about anger (see page 69), we learned one way to calm down. We can use a similar technique here to help better manage stress and respond more effectively to school pressure.

EXERCISE: BREATHING

If you have participated in chorus or choir, you may have had some practice working with your diaphragm (right above your belly). When you actually do full breathing into your diaphragm, it relaxes your body and calms you down. It slows down your heart rate, slows down your breathing, might make you a little light-headed (which is normal), and can make you a little sleepy. Let's give it a try.

Sit upright in a comfortable seat. Place one hand on your chest and the other hand on your belly. Push all the air out of your lungs, and then inhale deeply. When you do this, suck in as much air as you can and bring it not just into your chest, but down your lungs all the way into your belly (or diaphragm). When you inhale, you should see and feel your belly pushing out to accommodate the air you have inhaled. When you breathe out, you should see your belly get flatter again as the air leaves your body. Try experimenting with this and seeing if you can fill your belly up like a balloon with air when you inhale and let it all out when you exhale. You should feel your belly moving more than your chest. If you think you have it, you can try inhaling for five seconds and exhaling for seven seconds (if that's too much, try inhaling for three seconds and exhaling for five seconds). Do this for two minutes; try setting a timer so you can fully focus on breathing.

How do you feel? What did you notice? Many people feel a little calmer after this type of breathing. This is a great exercise to do before bed, before a big test, when you are feeling overwhelmed, or anytime during the day to give your body a little relaxation.

Friends can be the most important part of a person's life. While for many people friendships are a wonderful part of the teenage years, for others, making and keeping friends is extremely challenging. Perhaps you love your friends but you find you are always getting into arguments or constantly experiencing drama in your friend group. Or you are starting to feel uncomfortable with some of the things that your friends have been doing and aren't sure you want to continue to hang out with them. Or perhaps making friends has been tough and you often feel like an outsider among your peers. As wonderful as friends can be, it is important to have some skills to be able to manage the stressors that come with relationships, both with friends and in dating.

Working through Negative Thoughts

A big challenge of dealing with friends is our thoughts. What thoughts do you have about your friends? Here are some common thoughts that can come up related to friendships:

- "They won't like me if I don't do what they are doing."
- "She didn't respond to my text, so she must be mad at me."
- "I wasn't invited to hang out with everyone, so now I'm no longer cool."
- "If we go to different schools I will lose my friends."
- "I won't have anything if I don't have friends."
- "It's my fault that he's upset."

Remember the thinking mistakes we discussed in section 2 (see page 20)? These often come into play when dealing with friends. Can you identify any of those mistakes in the preceding list? The most common one is mind reading, as well as personalization and catastrophizing. Emotional reasoning often also comes up when we feel a strong emotion related to our friend and we believe our thoughts are true because of it. Remember, once we catch and label the thinking mistake, we want to translate it into an alternate thought that is more factual. Instead of "She didn't respond to my text so she must be mad at me," a more factual thought is "She didn't respond to my text." Let's see if you can catch any thinking mistakes you've had with your friends and create an alternate thought.

List three negative thoughts that you have related to your friends, label the thinking mistake, and come up with an alternate thought that is based on facts. See the example for some help. If you need to refresh your memory about thinking mistakes, see page 20.

Thought	Thinking Mistake	Alternate Thought
When I joined my friends, they stopped talking immediately, so obviously they were talking about me.	Mind reading	My friends stopped talking when I joined them, and they greeted me and asked how I was doing.

Setting Goals for Interaction

It can be difficult to know how to interact in a helpful way with friends or people we are dating. We may find ourselves arguing and not knowing what the argument is even about. We often don't focus on the goal we have when we interact with others, and so we end up saying or doing things that we later regret.

In most interactions, there are generally three underlying goals:

1. **Result:** What is the result you are trying to get out of the interaction? For example, do you want something from the other person (a favor, for them to understand you, money, time, etc.), or do you want to say no to something they have asked you or want you to do?

2. **Relationship:** How do you want your relationship with the other person to be? Specifically, how do you want them to feel about you when they interact with you? Do you want them to like you or feel love for you, trust you, respect you, enjoy your company, or feel happy?

3. **Respect for yourself:** This last goal is about how you feel about yourself during your interaction with someone else. Are you proud of yourself for the way you handled something? Are you confident, comfortable, in control, calm, assertive, gentle, respectful, or friendly?

Let's practice defining goals of an interaction with a friend. Let's use Lindsay, whose friend has not asked her to hang out lately but has been hanging out with other people. Here are Lindsay's goals in talking to her friend about this.

1. **Result:** To have her friend agree to include her more often.

2. **Relationship:** For her friend to respect and like her.

3. **Respect:** To stand up for herself and stay calm.

The next step is to prioritize which of these goals is most important to her. This could be different even with the same person depending on the situation. In this case, Lindsay has a hard time standing up for herself, so her order becomes: Respect, Result, Relationship. Now when Lindsay goes to talk to her friend, she can keep the most important goal in mind of standing up for herself and asking her friend to include her more often, instead of what Lindsay often does in these types of interactions, catering to what others want.

Often, people tend to either prioritize the relationship and how others feel about them too much, or prioritize their own respect of themselves and not consider others often enough. Think about which side you tend to be on. Whichever that is, an important practice is to try prioritizing the other side in some situations. Now let's try it.

EXERCISE: WHAT'S MY GOAL?

Think about a conversation or a situation coming up with a friend or someone you are dating.

_____

Now think about the different goals you have for that.

1. Result:
_____

2. Relationship:
_____

3. Respect:
_____

Great. Now rank your priorities for this particular interaction:

1.
_____

2.
_____

3.
_____

Going into the interaction with a priority goal in mind can help you stay on task, feel good about how you interacted with the other person, and help you manage your emotions in relationships.

Adapted from Rathus, Jill H., and Alec L. Miller. *DBT Skills Manual for Adolescents*. New York: The Guilford Press, 2014.

Dealing with Anxiety and Avoidance with Peers

Finally, let's focus on how anxiety can interfere with meeting new friends or dating. Think back to the section on anxiety (see page 77). Is there anything you are avoiding because of anxiety related to your peers? Let's break it down to help you not get so overwhelmed and avoid avoiding.

Let's use the example of asking someone new to hang out. In order to get more comfortable with doing that, what are some smaller steps to take to practice getting comfortable with it? Perhaps the first step would be saying yes when someone else asks you to hang out, then asking your best friend, who you are comfortable with, to hang out, then asking someone you are slightly less close with to hang out, then asking someone you have interacted with only a few times to hang out, and finally getting up the practice to ask someone new to hang out. Here's what that tracking practice sheet would look like based on what we discussed in section 4 (page 82).

Step	Anxiety Before (0 to 10)	Anxiety During (0 to 10)	Anxiety After (0 to 10)	Notes on Experience
Saying yes to someone	2	3	0	It wasn't hard.
Ask best friend	3	3	0	I was nervous right when I was asking.
Ask close friend	5	6	2	They said yes, so I felt better.
Ask friend	8	6	2	They said another time.
Ask someone new	10	10	4	They said yes!

It's your turn to think of a situation with your peers you have been avoiding because of anxiety. Create a chart and practice the steps to help face your anxiety.

EXERCISE: FACING YOUR ANXIETY WITH PEERS

Think about the situation and the different steps you would need to take. It may be all 10 steps, or it may be less. Pick the amount that works for you.

Situation to practice facing: _____

_____

Small steps toward the larger goal:

1. _____

2. _____

3. _____

4. _____

5. _____

6. _____

7. _____

8. _____

9. _____

10. _____

Now try the steps out, noting your anxiety before, during, and after and any observations or things you learned during your experience.

Step	Anxiety Before (0 to 10)	Anxiety During (0 to 10)	Anxiety After (0 to 10)	Notes on Experience

THE ROAD AHEAD

Congratulations—you made it through the workbook! Hopefully, you've noticed that if you take the time to do the exercises and put them into practice in your life, you will start to see the benefits. It really helps to take stock of your work from the book to see which exercises you found most helpful and what changes you are most proud of.

EXERCISE: CHOOSE MY TOOLBELT

Now that you have learned about the different exercises you can use to get closer to living the life you want, let's pick out the top five skills you want to make sure you continue to use on a regular basis. We discussed many tools in this book, and although all of them are valuable, it can be helpful to have a few you learn really well so that you're ready to use them anytime a challenging situation comes up. Take a look back through the book and write out the five skills that you found most helpful.

1. _____

2. _____

3. _____

4. _____

5. _____

Great. Now, in addition to these skills, think about which exercises you did that you thought were the most challenging or helpful. Pick three that jump out at you.

1. _____

2. _____

3. _____

How can you create something to keep with you that will help you remember these skills? Perhaps making a special note in your phone that reminds you or explains a short version of each skill? Some people make a kit to keep in their room and/or school bag with some of the materials that help them. For example, if the thought exercises were helpful, you could create a small notebook with the thinking mistakes and designated places to write alternate thoughts or ask yourself questions about your thoughts. If you are working on changing your behavior, you could carry a chart that sets your goal weekly and has your rewards planned out. If you are working on emotions, you might have some physical exercises to relax written down, keep a jump rope or other physical item to help you get active, or have your chart on facing anxiety with you. What is your plan for keeping these exercises with you to remember them easily and use them?

_____

_____

_____

_____

_____

Now that you have practiced ways to use skills in the important areas of your life and have a plan to move forward, it is your job to continue to use these skills on your own. In addition to using the skills you have just just listed, that may mean going back to different sections when you have specific problems with thoughts, behaviors, or emotions. It could mean coming back to this section to get some ideas for specific problems at home, in school, or with friends. Or it might mean sometimes going back through the book to see what could be helpful when new problems arise. This book is always here for you.

You have taken such a brave step in using this book. Remember that you are not alone in wanting to make your life better. Many others have been where you are, put these practices into place, and been much happier in life. You can do it too! Now take these exercises and go make some changes!

APPENDIX

Blank Exercises and Worksheets

You can find additional copies of these worksheets
at CallistoMediaBooks.com/CBTWorkbookForTeens.

EXERCISE: IDENTIFYING VALUES

Here are some values that may be important for you. Consider each one, and then
write in your own ideas on the blank lines at the end of the list:

- Be a good friend
- Put family first
- Volunteer and help others
- Be independent
- Enjoy life
- Always try to learn and grow
- Lead others
- Live a healthy lifestyle
- Have integrity
- Have honest and trusting relationships
- Be fair and treat people equally
- Act responsibly and reliably
- Be adventurous and try new things
- Be curious and nonjudgmental
- Accomplish goals

- _____

- _____

- _____

- _____

EXERCISE: PRIORITIZING VALUES

Pick three to five values that are the most important to you. Then rank them based on your current priorities. They can all be important, but consider the values you're most interested in working toward *right now*.

As you go through the workbook, keep these top values in mind. They will act as your guide for using certain skills for your needs, and for choosing behaviors to work on in the behavior section.

___ _____

___ _____

___ _____

___ _____

___ _____

Both exercises adapted from Rathus, Jill H., and Alec L. Miller. *DBT Skills Manual for Adolescents*. New York: The Guilford Press, 2015.

EXERCISE: SELF-ESTEEM ASSESSMENT

Here is an assessment of your self-esteem. Check whether each statement is never true, sometimes true, or often true.

	NEVER	SOMETIMES	OFTEN
1. I respect myself.	☐	☐	☐
2. I feel confident.	☐	☐	☐
3. I feel satisfied with myself.	☐	☐	☐
4. I believe I am good enough.	☐	☐	☐
5. I feel proud of myself.	☐	☐	☐
6. I believe I am just as worthy as other people.	☐	☐	☐
7. I feel comfortable in different settings.	☐	☐	☐
8. I feel useful.	☐	☐	☐
9. I meet my goals.	☐	☐	☐
10. I think positively about myself.	☐	☐	☐
11. I believe I am just as good as my friends.	☐	☐	☐
12. I can think of my good qualities.	☐	☐	☐

Adapted from Rosenberg, Morris. *Society and the Adolescent Self-Image*. Princeton, NJ: Princeton University Press, 1965.

EXERCISE: ANXIETY ASSESSMENT

Here is an assessment of your current anxiety level. Check whether each statement is never true, sometimes true, or often true.

	NEVER	SOMETIMES	OFTEN
1. I spend a lot of the day worrying.	☐	☐	☐
2. I have a hard time controlling my worry.	☐	☐	☐
3. I have a hard time calming down.	☐	☐	☐
4. I have trouble concentrating.	☐	☐	☐
5. I feel irritable.	☐	☐	☐
6. I have trouble falling or staying asleep at night.	☐	☐	☐
7. I avoid situations when I am anxious or worried.	☐	☐	☐
8. I worry about how others will view me.	☐	☐	☐
9. I try to do things perfectly.	☐	☐	☐
10. There are specific situations I avoid or experience a lot of fear in.	☐	☐	☐

Adapted from Spielberger, Charles D., C. D. Edwards, J. Montouri, and R. Lushene. "State-Trait Anxiety Inventory for Children." *PsycTESTS Dataset*, 1973. doi:10.1037/t06497-000.

EXERCISE: DEPRESSION ASSESSMENT

Here is an assessment to get a better sense of your level of depression. Choose whether each statement was never true, sometimes true, or often true **during the past week.**

DURING THE PAST WEEK	NEVER	SOMETIMES	OFTEN
1. I felt sad for most of the day.	☐	☐	☐
2. I felt irritable for most of the day.	☐	☐	☐
3. I couldn't enjoy things I usually enjoy.	☐	☐	☐
4. I had trouble concentrating.	☐	☐	☐
5. I wasn't very hungry.	☐	☐	☐
6. I slept more than usual.	☐	☐	☐
7. I felt like crying.	☐	☐	☐
8. I felt hopeless.	☐	☐	☐
9. I had trouble sleeping.	☐	☐	☐
10. I believed bad things were going to happen.	☐	☐	☐
11. I felt alone or lonely.	☐	☐	☐
12. I withdrew from friends or family.	☐	☐	☐
13. I had less energy than usual.	☐	☐	☐
14. I had less motivation than usual.	☐	☐	☐
15. I felt like nothing worked out the way I wanted.	☐	☐	☐

Adapted from Shahid, Azmeh, Kate Wilkinson, Shai Marcu, and Colin M. Shapiro, eds. "Center for Epidemiological Studies Depression Scale for Children (CES-DC)." In *STOP, THAT and One Hundred Other Sleep Scales*, 93–96. New York: Springer, 2011. doi:10.1007/978-1-4419-9893-4_16.

EXERCISE: BEING A SCIENTIST

Thought: _____

_____

Evidence For	Evidence Against
_____	_____
_____	_____
_____	_____
_____	_____

New hypothesis: _____

_____

EXERCISE: QUESTIONING YOUR THOUGHT

If it is difficult to come up with any evidence against your thought, you might need some prompting. The following is a list of questions you can ask yourself to help make the most accurate hypothesis about your thought. Using the example of the boy who was worried he would fail his math test and class, look at the questions and his answers that follow in italics. Then for each question, add your own answer about your own thought to the line underneath.

Is there a possible different outcome than the one you are worried about? *Yes, I could pass the test and pass the class, or even not do well on the test and pass the class.*

_____

_____

Am I making assumptions based on my emotions or confusing a feeling with a fact? (In other words, since my emotions are so strong, the thought must be true.) *Maybe.*

_____

What's the likely outcome based on what I already know has happened in past similar situations? *I won't fail but might get a C on the test.*

_____

_____

What is the percentage chance or the odds that my thought is true? 100 percent, 50 percent, 5 percent? *The chances of me actually failing are probably more like 30 percent.*

_____

Has there been a situation in the past similar to this that I got through? How did it turn out? *Yes, I have almost failed math tests before, but I have passed my math classes.*

_____

_____

What's the worst thing that could happen? *I could fail my math class.*

_____

_____

How would I cope with this worst thing happening? *I could go to summer school and make it up.*

_____

_____

Is there another point of view or perspective on this? *I have worked with my tutor and am getting better at math, and might not fail the test or the class.*

_____

_____

Can I see the future? *No.*

_____

What information might I be missing or forgetting about? *I can do extra credit to bring my grade up, and I got a B on the last test.*

_____

_____

It's your turn to try and pick one or two thoughts that are getting you stuck and use one or both of these techniques to reframe your thought.

Thought: _____

_____

Advantages of Having this Thought	**Disadvantages of Having this Thought**
_____	_____
_____	_____
_____	_____
_____	_____

Thought: _____

_____

EXERCISE: SELF-ESTEEM WORKOUT: CHALLENGING BELIEFS ABOUT YOURSELF

Pick one of the negative beliefs from the list on page 36, or another one along the same lines, that you have about yourself.

Write the belief here: _____

Now answer the following questions related to the belief:

Think of someone you know who you believe has the opposite trait. For example, if your thought is that you are unlovable or unworthy, think of someone who you believe to be lovable or worthy. Write their name here:

_____

What are some of the things they do that demonstrate these positive traits?

_____

_____

If your close friend or family member were having the same negative thoughts about themselves, what would you tell them?

_____

_____

What would your close friend or family member say you have done that is evidence that you have these positive traits (being lovable or worthy)?

_____

_____

Now list some behaviors you can practice to help demonstrate that you are the opposite of your belief. These are things you would do if you believed the opposite were true (that you were worthy or lovable). For example, if you thought you were unworthy, acting worthy might involve asking for things that you have earned, or practicing appearing confident with an upright posture and holding your head up high. If your belief is that you are crazy, some practices might be to talk more about your thoughts with others, try telling yourself that what you are thinking and feeling makes sense, or notice when others might be feeling the same way as you.

_____

_____

_____

_____

_____

EXERCISE: NOTICING THOUGHTS AND URGES

For this exercise, pick a thought that has resulted in an action you did not want. For example, thoughts such as "I hate myself," "I really want to eat this dessert," "He will never go out with me," "I don't want to go to school today," or "I'm ugly," could all result in different urges or actions. These might include punching a wall or avoiding social situations, eating something you later regret, not making eye contact with the person you like, pretending to be sick to stay home, or frowning throughout the day.

Pick a negative thought that has resulted in an action that you did not want:

_____

What do you notice or how do you feel when you have this thought?

_____

Now add the words "I'm having the thought that" in front of that thought, and write out the sentence:

_____

_____

What do you notice or how do you feel when you have this new thought?

_____

Now add "I'm noticing that I'm having the thought that" in front of the original thought:

_____

_____

What do you notice or how do you feel when you have this new thought?

_____

Now let's try this with an urge.

Write an urge you are having:

_____

Now add "I'm noticing that I'm having the urge to" in front of the urge:

_____

_____

How did you feel when thinking this way about an urge?

_____

Simply adding these phrases can help you step out of your automatic thinking style and start to see your thoughts just as thoughts, instead of believing they are true and acting on them. It can also put some distance between your urges and your actions. You can try this simple practice when you find yourself continuing to automatically act on urges.

EXERCISE: JUST A WORD

Another way to start recognizing the separation between your thoughts and actions is to remember that a thought is just a bunch of letters that we form with sounds. We give our thoughts so much meaning that we forget they are just a string of sounds put together. Take the word "bowl." Set a timer for 30 seconds, then say "bowl" over and over until the timer goes off. What did you notice?

_____

When I do this, I tend to find that the sound of the "o" starts to sound weird. It stops sounding like a real word, and more like just a silly sound. It starts to take away the meaning of the word.

Now take one of the core negative beliefs you picked about yourself in section 2, and pick the key word (unworthy, unattractive, unlovable, etc.).

_____

Now set your timer for one minute, and keep saying that word out loud over and over until the timer goes off. What did you notice?

_____

How is this different than how you usually respond to this word or thought?

_____

Recognizing that some thoughts are just silly sounds can help you detach from the meaning of the word. This can give you the freedom to *choose* to act however you want, which is not necessarily based on how your thoughts tell you to act. Try this exercise again the next time you find yourself having a thought that gives you an unhelpful urge.

Write out the three to five values you identified in section 1, in order of importance:

_____

_____

_____

_____

_____

Pick the one that you want to start working on now.

_____

Let's use "be independent" as an example. The next step is to think about a concrete goal that supports this value. So if the value is being independent, a few goals might be getting an after-school job, doing your homework without your parents reminding you, doing your own laundry, getting a driver's license, or getting into college. What is your goal going to be?

_____

_____

Now let's think through all the steps that it will take to accomplish your goal. Let's say your goal was to get a job. You would have to break it down into smaller steps that might be (1) Googling options for local jobs, (2) picking out a few jobs you are interested in, (3) figuring out how you can apply to the jobs you want, (4) applying for the jobs, (5) interviewing for the jobs, (6) starting the job. And all of these can actually be broken down into even smaller steps. So now take your goal and break it down into 5–10 smaller steps.

_____

_____

_____

_____

_____

_____

_____

_____

Great work. Now that you have broken it down, what's the first step you will take?

_____

Adapted from Linehan, Marsha. *DBT® Skills Training Handouts and Worksheets*. New York: The Guilford Press, 2015.

EXERCISE: BREAKING THROUGH BARRIERS

Write out the steps from your earlier goal and fill in the chart for possible barriers and solutions, using the chart on page 49 as a guide.

Step toward Goal	Possible Barriers	Solutions to Barriers

In order to better understand and start to notice the behaviors you want to change, it is helpful to collect data on when and how often you do them, which also helps you start noticing the urge before the behavior is completed. Over the next two days, use this sheet to track the three behaviors you want to change.

Behavior	Number	Times of Day	Place	With Who

Let's write out up to three behaviors that you want to change now, and think of two possible alternative positive behaviors, or replacement behaviors.

Behavior to Decrease	Possible Replacement Behavior 1	Possible Replacement Behavior 2

Now you have some ideas for what you can begin substituting for some of your unwanted behaviors. You may also already have some behaviors you know you want to increase, like exercising more often, eating healthier, getting up earlier, going out more, spending more time with your family, or others. What behaviors would you like to increase?

_____

_____

_____

Consider some behaviors or situations that you avoid doing because they make you anxious. Avoiding them long term may go against the values you have, so it may be important to face these fears. If any behaviors apply, add them to your list below.

_____

_____

_____

List out some rewards you can create for yourself. If you find yourself getting stuck, think about the things you enjoy doing most.

_____

_____

_____

_____

_____

_____

_____

In addition to rewards, making a commitment to other people can be very helpful for following through on something. These should be people you trust who will hold you to your commitment and can celebrate with you when you accomplish your goal. Who are some of those people?

_____

_____

EXERCISE: YOUR FIRST COMMITTED ACTION PLAN

Priority value: _____

Goal you already set related to this value:

_____

New behaviors to work on in line with this value (these could be your new alternative behaviors, behaviors to increase, or behaviors related to anxiety):

- ■ _____

- ■ _____

- ■ _____

To make it easier for you to practice these new behaviors, it helps to turn them into concrete, specific goals. We will set goals for one week at a time. For example, if the behavior you are adding is exercising, you might set the goal of going to the gym two times this week. Or if you are going to wait five minutes before texting people back, you might give yourself the goal of doing this three times a day for a week. If you are working on spending time in bigger groups, you might set the goal of finding one or two group activities to do this week. Go ahead and make very specific weekly goals for the three behaviors so that you will be able to say easily if you accomplished them or not.

Goals this week:

- Behavior 1:

  _____

- Behavior 2:

  _____

- Behavior 3:

  _____

Great! Now, go back to the goal you initially set related to this value (see page 125). Let's pick the first two steps. In my example of getting a job, those are (1) Googling local options for jobs, and (2) considering these options. Therefore the goal would be to find time to do those two steps sometime in the next week, and we would add that to our list.

Value goals:

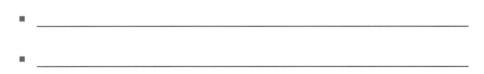

- _____

- _____

You now have five goals to work on this week: three goals related to behaviors you want to change, and two smaller steps in line with a bigger goal. Now we need to commit to a day and time to work on each of these goals and create rewards for each. Fill out your weekly committed action plan for this week:

Week Of: _____

Value: _____

Goal	Time, Day/Date I Plan to Do This	Person Holding Me Accountable	Reward I Get

Fill in this chart if you had any barriers that got in the way of your goals.

Goal	Barriers	Possible Solution to Barriers

Take some time to fill out your weekly committed action plan for week two.

Week Of: _____

Value: _____

Goal	Time, Day/Date I Plan to Do This	Person Holding Me Accountable	Reward I Get

EXERCISE: RELEASING ANGER MENTALLY

Anger can lead to thoughts or urges within you that you just need to get out. You may be tempted to get them out by yelling at someone, telling them how much they have hurt you, telling them how much you are suffering, or trying to get revenge. However, these tactics could really interfere with your goals and probably act against your values.

One way to release these strong feelings of anger without doing damage is to write them down in a letter that you never give the person. You can write out what you want to say and all the reasons you are angry. Don't hold back! This will provide a sense of release and relief. Then throw the letter away, lock it in a drawer, password protect it, or let it go in some other way. See how you feel after you write out all the emotion without acting on your urges.

_____

_____

_____

_____

_____

EXERCISE: WHAT'S UNDERNEATH YOUR ANGER?

Below, spend a few minutes writing about the things that usually make you angry. See if there might be some alternative causes to your anger besides not getting what you want. If these emotions are sadness or fear, you can use some of the exercises in the following sections to help manage them.

The last thing I got angry about was _____.

I was angry because _____.

I usually get angry (at who) _____

(in what situations) _____

(time of day) _____

(when I think about) _____.

Possible other emotions that could be underneath my anger are:

_____

_____

_____

EXERCISE: WHEN YOUR SADNESS FEELS TOO DEEP

As we discussed, emotions are like waves. If you fight the emotion or run away, it will drag you down. If you let it engulf you, it might swallow you whole. Instead, the goal is to ride the emotional wave. To do this, you need to use mindfulness to observe your emotions. Try this exercise with your sadness.

Pay attention to your emotion as though you are an observer not attached to the experience. How does sadness feel in your body? How do you know you are sad? Do you feel something in your throat? In your chest? In your head? In your stomach? What is the energy like in your body? Do you feel the urge to cry? Any other urges? How long are these sensations lasting? Are they changing in strength or staying consistent? What else do you notice about your emotion? When was the last time you felt this way? How long did it last? Try acknowledging that this emotion is here right now. Whatever it is, it's already here. Nothing to do, nothing to change, just notice how things are in this moment. Remember that things are always changing, that things will be different in the next moment, and this is just how this moment feels.

Take some time to reflect after that exercise. What did you notice?

_____

Is this similar or different to how you usually respond to your sadness?

_____

Often, when people have an extreme emotion, it is hard to remember that you might feel different, that you have ever felt different, or that sadness is just one emotion you have. Sometimes we make it seem like there is no other option but to dwell in an emotion or to get stuck in it, and declare it our worst enemy. But the reality is that you can treat it like a toothache, a stubbed toe, a feeling of excitement, the sound of a song you like, or any other experience. It's not more or less important, it is just one of many. Taking a step back like this to observe the sadness can help us get some distance from it and not feel like it defines us or has full control.

Adapted from Segal, Zindel V., J. Mark, G. Williams, and John D. Teasdale. *Mindfulness-Based Cognitive Therapy for Depression*. New York: The Guilford Press, 2013.

EXERCISE: GET MOVING

Activity Type	Depression Before (0 to 10)	Depression After (0 to 10)	Notes on Experience

EXERCISE: GETTING TO THE BOTTOM OF ANXIETY

What situation are you worried about and what are your worries?

_____

_____

If this were true, what would that mean to you?

_____

And if that were the case, what would that mean to you?

_____

And if that were true, what would that mean about you?

_____

Remember our core belief practice in section 2? Often these anxious thoughts are linked to one of those core beliefs. Before moving forward, go back to page 37 and try the exercise about core beliefs.

Adapted from Beck, Judith S. *Cognitive Behavior Therapy Basics and Beyond.* New York: The Guilford Press, 2011.

EXERCISE: AVOIDING

Situation to practice facing: _____

_____

Small steps toward the larger goal:

1. _____

2. _____

3. _____

4. _____

5. _____

6. _____

7. _____

8. _____

9. _____

10. _____

Now, try the steps out. Each time you try a step, it helps to keep some data. Rate your anxiety before, during, and after from 0 (no anxiety) to 10 (highest anxiety). Use the following sheet to track your progress.

Step	Anxiety Before (0 to 10)	Anxiety During (0 to 10)	Anxiety After (0 to 10)	Notes on Experience

What's a reasonable goal?

├─────────────────────────────────┼─────────────────────────────────┤

Now let's think of two other areas of conflict where you and your parents disagree on privileges. Complete the following chart with markers for where you and your parents are. Then establish the middle point, and set a new goal to talk to them about it.

├─────────────────────────────────┼─────────────────────────────────┤

├─────────────────────────────────┼─────────────────────────────────┤

EXERCISE: REINFORCING SIBLINGS

Let's list three behaviors that you would like your siblings to do. Remember, if it is a behavior you would like them to *stop* doing, phrase it as an alternative behavior to increase instead of an admonishment, such as "Please ask before you borrow something," instead of "Never take my stuff without asking."

_____

_____

_____

Now let's think about what rewards you could give them for each behavior.

_____

_____

_____

Where will your space be?

_____

Now let's make a list of items to have ready or keep in this space.

- ▪ _____

- ▪ _____

- ▪ _____

- ▪ _____

- ▪ _____

- ▪ _____

- ▪ _____

- ▪ _____

- ▪ _____

- ▪ _____

Write out some of the things that are part of who you are here.

_____

_____

_____

Look at the different slices of the following pie chart. Fill in school/grades, as well as some of these other aspects of yourself in the even slices.

EXERCISE: SETTING GOALS FOR BEING IN CLASS

List out three behaviors that you plan to work on improving in classes and with your teachers. Remember to write out the specific goal for the week, barriers, solution to barriers, and the reward you will give yourself, just like we did in section 3.

Weekly Goal	Possible Barriers	Solutions to Barriers	Reward

List three negative thoughts that you have related to your friends, label the thinking mistake, and come up with an alternate thought that is based on facts. See the example on page 96 for some help. If you need to refresh your memory about thinking mistakes, see page 20.

Thought	Thinking Mistake	Alternate Thought

Think about a conversation or a situation coming up with a friend or someone you are dating.

_____

_____

Now think about the different goals you have for that.

1. **Result:** _____

2. **Relationship:** _____

3. **Respect:** _____

Great. Now rank your priorities for this particular interaction:

1. _____

2. _____

3. _____

Going into the interaction with a priority goal in mind can help you stay on task, feel good about how you interacted with the other person, and help you manage your emotions in relationships.

Adapted from Rathus, Jill H., and Alec L. Miller. *DBT Skills Manual for Adolescents*. New York: The Guilford Press, 2014.

EXERCISE: FACING YOUR ANXIETY WITH PEERS

Think about the situation and the different steps you would need to take. It may be all 10 steps, or it may be less. Pick the amount that works for you.

Situation to practice facing: _____

_____

Small steps toward the larger goal:

1. _____

2. _____

3. _____

4. _____

5. _____

6. _____

7. _____

8. _____

9. _____

10. _____

Now try the steps out, noting your anxiety before, during, and after and any observations or things you learned during your experience.

Step	Anxiety Before (0 to 10)	Anxiety During (0 to 10)	Anxiety After (0 to 10)	Notes on Experience

EXERCISE: CHOOSE MY TOOLBELT

Now that you have learned about the different exercises you can use to get closer to living the life you want, let's pick out the top five skills you want to make sure you continue to use on a regular basis.

1. _____

2. _____

3. _____

4. _____

5. _____

Great. Now, in addition to these skills, think about which exercises you did that you thought were the most challenging or helpful. Pick three that jump out at you.

1. _____

2. _____

3. _____

What is your plan for keeping these exercises with you to remember them easily and use them?

_____

_____

_____

_____

_____

MORE RESOURCES

Association for Behavioral and Cognitive Therapies' Find a Therapist directory: http://www
.findcbt.org/xFAT.

Biegel, Gina M. *Stress Reduction Workbook for Teens: Mindfulness Skills to Help You Deal with
Stress*. Oakland, CA: Instant Help Books, 2017.

McKay, Matthew. *Thoughts & Feelings: Taking Control of Your Mood and Your Life*. Oakland, CA:
New Harbinger Publications, 2012.

National Suicide Prevention Lifeline: 1-800-273-8255

Pincus, Donna, Jill T. Ehrenreich, Sara Golden Mattis, and Donna Pincus. *Mastery of Anxiety
and Panic for Adolescents: Riding the Wave*. Oxford, UK: Oxford University Press, 2008.

The Trevor Project (hotline and chat support for LGBTQ teens): 1-866-488-7386

INDEX

ABOUT THE AUTHOR

 Dr. Rachel L. Hutt is a licensed clinical psychologist and co-founder of MindWell NYC, a group private practice in Manhattan, New York. She works with children, teens, and parents on incorporating Cognitive Behavioral Therapy and Dialectical Behavioral Therapy skills in their daily lives to help them build the kind of life they want to live.